NEW DIRECTIONS FOR PROGRAM EVALUATION
A Publication of the American Evaluation Association

Nick L. Smith, *Syracuse University*
EDITOR-IN-CHIEF

Inspectors General: A New Force in Evaluation

Michael Hendricks
Independent Consultant

Michael F. Mangano
Office of Evaluation and Inspections

William C. Moran
Office of Evaluation and Inspections

EDITORS

Number 48, Winter 1990

JOSSEY-BASS INC., PUBLISHERS
San Francisco

INSPECTORS GENERAL: A NEW FORCE IN EVALUATION
Michael Hendricks, Michael F. Mangano, William C. Moran (eds.)
New Directions for Program Evaluation, no. 48
Nick L. Smith, Editor-in-Chief

Microfilm copies of issues and articles are available in 16mm and 35mm,
as well as microfiche in 105mm, through University Microfilms Inc., 300
North Zeeb Road, Ann Arbor, Michigan 48106.

LC 85-644749   ISSN 0164-7989   ISBN 1-55542-814-2

NEW DIRECTIONS FOR PROGRAM EVALUATION is part of The Jossey-Bass
Higher and Adult Education and Social and Behavioral Science Series
and is published quarterly by Jossey-Bass Inc., Publishers (publication
number USPS 449-050).

EDITORIAL CORRESPONDENCE should be sent to the Editor-in-Chief,
Nick L. Smith, School of Education, Syracuse University, 330 Huntington
Hall, Syracuse, New York 13244-2340.

Printed on acid-free paper in the United States of America.

CONTENTS

EDITORS' NOTES

One of the most interesting and controversial developments in program evaluation today is the increasing role of evaluations conducted by the federal Offices of Inspectors General (OIGs). Since OIGs were first placed into a few federal agencies over ten years ago, they have spread to almost all agencies. Recently, in fact, Congress forced the president to agree, over his objections, to the creation of an independent OIG within the Central Intelligence Agency. This indicates that OIGs have become one of the dominant players at the federal level and one of the offices Congress believes, whether accurately or not, can oversee federal programs most effectively.

At the beginning these OIGs conducted mainly the financial audits and criminal investigations with which most people still associate OIGs. However, there is a definite and increasing trend for OIGs to perform a third type of activity: program inspections, which, by some criteria, are akin to program evaluations. Recent unpublished data show that OIGs in at least eight federal agencies currently have an inspection activity, three other OIGs have a similar activity, and two more OIGs intend to develop one. Thus, at least thirteen federal agencies now have or soon will have OIGs conducting evaluation-type activities.

However, most evaluators know very little, if anything, about these OIG evaluators. Who are these people? Do they really do evaluations? How do they do them? How well? And, perhaps most important, what does their work mean for other evaluations and other evaluators? In other words, is evaluation by these OIGs a healthy direction for growth or an ominous sign for the future?

Timeliness and Importance of the Topic of OIGs

This topic is timely and important for at least six reasons. First, the growth of OIG evaluations is undeniable. We mentioned above the increasing number of federal agencies with active OIG evaluation offices. Also increasing is the number of staff within each of these offices (the number of OIG evaluators within the U.S. Department of Health and Human Services [HHS], for example, has almost tripled—from 50 to 140—in the past five years). Furthermore, OIG budgets have also increased. In a time of scarce federal dollars, OIG evaluators are relatively well funded and are still one of the "fair-haired" children of the present administration.

Second, and closely related, while OIG evaluation resources have been increasing, those for other evaluations have been shrinking. At the Department of Justice, for example, every evaluation unit in the department (except for the FBI) is being consolidated into a new evaluation unit within the OIG.

Third, OIG evaluations are becoming quite visible. It is not unusual for OIG evaluations, for example, to be the focus of congressional hearings or to appear in major newspapers, on network news programs, in news magazines, or on radio programs. As a result of this exposure, OIG evaluations may be defining, for many audiences, just exactly what is an "evaluation."

Fourth, OIGs represent a unique organizational arrangement, being both "inside" their respective agencies (reporting to the secretaries), and "outside" at the same time (also reporting, equally and independently, to Congress). The evaluation literature has discussed the ideal organizational arrangement for evaluators (Chelimsky, 1985), and OIGs represent one interesting variation to study.

Fifth, OIGs practice "advocacy evaluation," an approach favored by Sonnichsen (1988) and others as a way for evaluators to champion their findings and recommendations. As relatively well-funded and independent practitioners of this approach, OIGs might prove to be informative case studies of the potentials of advocacy evaluation under the best possible circumstances.

Finally, OIG evaluations may eventually affect evaluations at lower levels of government and in nonprofit and private organizations. If OIG evaluations are ultimately judged to be successful, more and more state and local officials, as well as administrators of nongovernmental organizations, can be expected to create similar functions in their own agencies.

Concerns About OIG Evaluations

Obviously, OIG evaluations are an interesting development. However, we also called them controversial, and they are. By no means do all observers believe that OIG evaluations represent a healthy direction for growth. Quite the contrary, some observers see serious dangers in this direction, and they might well call OIG evaluations an ominous sign for the future.

Newcomer (1989, p. 60) states these concerns most directly: "Urge upper management to transfer all evaluation responsibilities to the Inspector General (IG) in their agency. Ferreting out fraud and abuse is much more appealing to politicians than analyzing program operations and impact. Once evaluation has been transferred to the IG's office, then one can simply let the IG staff finish off the job. The IG can convince any political appointee that auditing really is evaluation, and evaluation really is auditing, and auditing is actually auditing, and evaluation is actually nothing more to speak of."

Others might express their concerns differently, but we believe it is fair to say that well-respected evaluators such as Newcomer hold very different opinions on the contributions and implications of OIG evaluations for the evaluation profession. That controversy is part of what makes this topic so interesting and part of why we are so pleased to present this volume, *Inspectors General: A New Force in Evaluation.*

Overview of This Volume

In order to capture the spirit of the different opinions presented here, we have deliberately structured the volume within a debate or point-counterpoint format. We offer an initial overview chapter, three "pro" case studies by heads of OIG evaluation offices, and two "con" or questioning chapters by respected outside evaluators. For all chapters, we have encouraged each author to present his own perspective in the most favorable light, much as speakers would in an actual debate.

In Part One, William C. Moran presents the history of OIGs and their growing involvement in evaluation ("inspections"). He also presents previously unpublished data on the organizational location, staff qualifications, scope of work, and standards used by OIG evaluators.'Certain of these data suggest that OIG inspections fall into two camps: *systemic* looks at broadly defined issues or programs and *targeted* looks at narrowly focused policies, issues, or organizations. Moran concludes by discussing key characteristics of inspections across federal OIGs, some common lessons that might interest other evaluators, and questions raised by this new form of evaluation.

Part Two contains the three favorable or "pro" case studies conducted by heads of different federal OIG evaluation offices. In Chapter Two, Michael F. Mangano presents inspections at HHS. By almost every measure, these systemic inspections at HHS most closely resemble more "traditional" evaluations. Mangano discusses the topics his office studies, the methods they use, the ways they ensure quality control, and the products they produce. He then offers four different ways that their inspections have improved HHS, and he postulates six reasons for this effectiveness.

In Chapter Three, Charlie Hall and Johnnie Frazier present a somewhat different type of OIG inspection at another domestic agency, the U.S. Department of Commerce. These inspections are occasionally systemic, but they are usually more narrowly targeted than those at HHS. Often a prelude to a more detailed management audit or investigation, these inspections appear to be less like traditional evaluations and more like a new hybrid of evaluation and auditing. As such, Hall and Frazier's discussion of the inspections process (including unannounced visits to sites) is especially interesting.

In Chapter Four, William F. Vance looks inside a military setting and presents yet a third type of OIG inspection, as conducted at the U.S. Department of Defense. Unlike the situations at HHS and Commerce, the centralized Defense OIG must coexist with other OIGs from each of the separate military services. Perhaps it is not surprising, then, since the topics to be studied must be chosen with such care, that the inspections planning process is so important to this office. Vance discusses this planning process, and the resultant steps, in some detail.

The volume then reverses perspective in Part Three, with two chapters representing the questioning or "con" view of OIG inspections. In Chapter Five, David S. Cordray steps back from the details of the inspections process and asks three basic questions: (1) What should the overall portfolio of all evaluation activities look like? (2) What, if any, of this portfolio can OIG inspections provide? (3) What do the current OIG successes imply for the rest of the portfolio? Cordray frankly concludes that if OIGs' role in evaluation continues to increase and if non-OIG evaluation resources continue to decline, "program evaluation will be retarded rather than enhanced by the presence of the OIGs."

In Chapter Six, Richard C. Sonnichsen continues this questioning by raising the following concerns about inspections: (1) *purposes* (Do OIGs' "extreme emphasis on the funding and accountability of government programs" bias which programs and issues are studied?), (2) *focuses* (Can OIG evaluators serve both the administration and Congress? What are the implications of OIGs' inherent need for publicity?), and (3) *methodologies* (Are OIG staff sufficiently qualified? Do time pressures preclude using proper methods?). Nonetheless, Sonnichsen concludes with a call for diversity in the evaluation profession and a list of lessons we might learn from OIG inspections.

Conclusion

Our goal in presenting this volume is neither to advocate nor to campaign against evaluation activities as currently practiced by federal OIGs. Instead, our goal is to publicize a development that is important now and will become even more important in the future, but about which most evaluators seem to be completely unaware.

To reach this goal we have used a point-counterpoint format to raise as many issues as possible for readers to consider on their own. We hope the format works, and we hope the dialogue continues on this important topic.

Michael Hendricks
Michael F. Mangano
William C. Moran
Editors

References

Chelimsky, E. "Old Patterns and New Directions in Program Evaluation." In E. Chelimsky (ed.), *Program Evaluation: Patterns and Directions.* Washington, D.C.: American Society for Public Administration, 1985.
Newcomer, K. E. "Ten Ways to Kill Evaluation." *Bureaucrat,* 1989, *18,* 59-60.
Sonnichsen, R. C. "Advocacy Evaluation: A Model for Internal Evaluation Offices." *Evaluation and Program Planning,* 1988, *11,* 141-148.

Michael Hendricks has recently moved to New Delhi, India, where he continues as an independent consultant in program evaluation and planning, organizational development, and technical assistance and training.

Michael F. Mangano is the deputy inspector general, Office of Evaluation and Inspections, Office of Inspector General, U.S. Department of Health and Human Services. In the last five years, he has overseen over 270 evaluation studies, given numerous interviews to television, radio, and the print media, and regularly testified before Congress.

William C. Moran is the HHS regional inspector general, Office of Evaluation and Inspections, Chicago. Over the past five years, he has chaired an HHS OIG Procedures Committee that developed the procedures, standards, and methodology for the HHS OIG inspections function.

PART ONE

Overview of Inspections by the Offices of Inspectors General

A new form of program evaluation, called inspections, is changing the evaluation landscape in a number of federal agencies.

Evaluation Within the Federal Offices of Inspectors General

William C. Moran

An important evaluation movement has been developing in the federal government for the past decade, but it has received only scant notice. This movement has significant implications for the way evaluation is conducted in the executive branch, so it is now time to name the movement and to discuss its implications.

The movement in question is called "inspections" and it can be found inside the Offices of Inspectors General (OIGs) in most large federal agencies. It is a significant movement because (1) the staff involved produce reports that are read and make recommendations that are seriously debated by policymakers in the executive and legislative branches of the federal government, (2) the staff currently define themselves collectively as a short-term evaluation mechanism that understands some of the pitfalls of traditional program evaluation, and (3) the movement is still maturing and looking to different disciplines for guidance and boundaries.

Ever since Congress established the first statutory Inspector General in 1976, there has been a gradual yet definitive shift in oversight and evaluation responsibilities in many federal agencies. This chapter describes this shift by examining two broad themes: (1) a political science theme that oversight and evaluation functions have organizationally changed within federal agencies over the past decade and (2) an evaluation methodology theme that innovative practices have occurred that might be useful for other program evaluators. The chapter concludes with a set of questions about the implications of this decade-old movement. Overall, the goal is to provide essential facts and to raise sufficient questions about this inspections movement so that a healthy dialogue might begin in the broader evaluation community.

NEW DIRECTIONS FOR PROGRAM EVALUATION, no. 48, Winter 1990 © Jossey-Bass Inc., Publishers

Background

Disenchantment with Traditional Evaluation. By the mid 1970s, the role of planning and evaluation appeared to be well-ensconced in the federal bureaucracy. The assistant secretary for Planning and Evaluation and the research units in the major program components seemed to have adequate funds to carry out traditional social science evaluation. The main characteristics of this traditional evaluation were outside contracts with consulting firms and universities, rigorous research methodology, use of large amounts of money, production of thick reports, and approximately two years' completion time for each evaluation.

By the late 1970s, attitudes within the bureaucracy shifted somewhat regarding the role and usefulness of evaluations. Policymakers were dissatisfied with the length of time that it took to get answers to questions they asked of evaluators. There were also questions about the types of studies being conducted and their relevance to current policy discussions. Overall, policymakers wanted common sense answers to common sense questions in a timely fashion.

These questions about the usefulness and role of evaluation within the bureaucracy became more serious when the Reagan administration took office in 1981. First, the budget became a focal point for discussion and debate. Top-level managers wanted to know the budget implications on all issues. This budget focus certainly applied equally to the issues included in any program evaluation. It also meant that the administration had to make decisions about which types of federal activities, including evaluation activities, would be cut in order to meet reduced budget targets.

Second, the new administration placed increased emphasis on fraud and abuse not only for budgetary reasons but also because they wanted to ensure that only those persons certified as eligible would be served by federal programs. This emphasis, too, had implications for the type of evaluations to be given high priority.

Third, the administration believed that the federal government was collecting too much data from states, localities, and the general public. Their reaction took the form of block grants, paperwork reduction, and simplified reporting, all steps that had implications for the federal evaluation community both in terms of defining the federal evaluation responsibility and in terms of the type and amount of data that evaluators could collect from state and local grantees.

Finally, the administration recognized the need to be objective about evaluation results. Perhaps due in part to the post-Watergate mentality of ensuring honesty and ethical behavior, policymakers strongly believed in the need to ensure that those conducting a study had no vested interest in the outcomes of that study, regardless of whether the study was conducted by agency staff or by outside contractors.

These questions and attitudes in the early 1980s did, in fact, have a noticeable impact on evaluation staff in the non-Defense Department agencies throughout the 1980s. The U.S. General Accounting Office (1988) reported a 22 percent decrease in professional staff in agency evaluation units between 1980 and 1984. In addition, funds for evaluation purposes decreased by 37 percent during that same period, with further reductions between 1984 and 1988.

For someone concerned about the role of program evaluation in the federal government, the diminution of evaluation staff raises questions about the availability of information on program policies and performance. Yet, to focus solely on these evaluation cutbacks may not give a well-rounded picture of what was actually occurring during the years 1980–1988. Another piece of the evaluation kaleidoscope needs to be looked at, namely, the inspections function within OIG.

Growth of OIGs and Inspections. Prior to OIGs, internal oversight was performed by auditors who were located in the operating components of each agency being audited as well as in an Office of Audit that reported to an assistant secretary. External oversight was conducted by the responsible congressional committee and by the General Accounting Office (GAO). The Office of Management and Budget (OMB) also played an oversight role.

During the mid 1970s, the aftermath of the Watergate scandal and the rapid increase in the federal budget contributed to Congress's need to create a different type of oversight function. They wanted a consolidated oversight office within the major federal agencies that would know what was going on but would not be accountable solely to the head of any agency being audited. Thus, they created OIGs.

Over the past fourteen years, Congress has established OIGs in sixty-seven federal agencies, twenty-four of which presently require presidential appointment of the Inspector General (IG). The vast majority of these offices were established by the Inspector General Act of 1978 and the Inspector General Act Amendments of 1988. Table 1 lists the twenty-four active agencies (and one now defunct agency) requiring presidential appointments and the dates the agencies were established.

The OIGs are required to have independent and objective units to (1) promote the economy, efficiency, and effectiveness of federal operations and (2) prevent and detect fraud, waste, and mismanagement. In carrying out these responsibilities, the IGs are to report regularly both to their respective agency heads and to Congress. The Inspector General Act intended that this dual reporting relationship ensure public disclosure of IG findings and IG independence from agency pressures (U.S. Dept. of the Treasury, 1988).

For some of the very reasons that traditional evaluation activity was being questioned, OIGs were being created and nurtured. OIG staff are supposed to find ways to save money, to recommend program efficiency

Table 1. Presidentially Appointed Inspectors General

Federal Agency	Date OIG Established
Health and Human Services	1976
(formerly Health, Education, and Welfare)	
Energy	1977
Agriculture	1978
Commerce	1978
Housing and Urban Development	1978
Interior	1978
Labor	1978
Transportation	1978
General Services Administration	1978
National Aeronautics and Space Administration	1978
Small Business Administration	1978
Veterans Administration	1978
Environmental Protection Agency	1978
Community Services Administration[a]	1978
Education	1979
Agency for International Development	1981
Defense	1982
Railroad Retirement Board	1983
State	1985
United States Information Agency	1986
Justice	1988
Treasury	1988
Federal Emergency Management Agency	1988
Nuclear Regulatory Commission	1988
Office of Personnel Management	1988

[a]This agency no longer exists.

and effectiveness improvements, to expose fraud and abuse, to simplify administrative reporting requirements, to be objective in looking for solutions, and to accomplish these tasks in a manner and time frame that policymakers can use in their day-to-day decision making.

Organizationally, OIGs are each supposed to have two offices: one to perform internal and external *audits* of agency expenditures and the other to conduct criminal, civil, and administrative *investigations*. The audits are to be carried out by auditors and accountants with financial management backgrounds, and the investigations by persons trained in law enforcement, such as former police officers and Federal Bureau of Investigation and Internal Revenue Service agents. For the most part, these audit and investigations staffs already existed in some fashion within the federal agencies and were simply consolidated within the newly created OIGs.

Some IGs decided that, in addition to the two functions of audit and investigations, they would also establish a third separate and distinct function. This function, known as inspections, is basically an evaluation activity, with studies that range from tightly focused compliance reviews to broadly directed systemic surveys. Some inspections examine the extent to which individual federal programs or installations are complying with applicable laws, regulations, and policies, while other inspections determine how entire programs might be amended or redirected.

These inspections, which are usually short-term (from two to six months) and employ a variety of methodologies, are conducted by OIG staff from a variety of different disciplines, including evaluators, policy analysts, program analysts, statisticians, management analysts, engineers, military officers, foreign service officers, auditors, journalists, physicians, and investigators.

In order to clearly understand inspections, it is useful to examine the differences among the three functions of investigations, audits, and inspections. An investigation focuses on a single provider of a service to determine if there is criminal or civil wrongdoing; an audit focuses on an agency or group of providers to determine if federal money has been spent appropriately; an inspection evaluates the broader management of an entity or examines the policies, operations, regulations, or legislative implications of a given issue.

Richard P. Kusserow, the current Inspector General at Health and Human Services (HHS), makes the following analogy: Investigations are like the artillery because they use big guns against a given target; audits are like the infantry since they are more personnel intensive and have to systematically move from one provider, or group of providers, to the next; and inspections are like a cavalry that is smaller in number than the opposition but is sent out to scout the opponent's overall position in order either to engage in a limited encounter or to report back and draw up a larger battle plan (personal communication, n.d.).

Inspections as a New Evaluation Activity

Among the twenty-four active agencies that have a presidentially appointed IG, eight have an inspections function, four have a similar function, and one intends to develop an inspections function. Those agencies that have an inspection's function are responsible for approximately 75 percent of all federal expenditures. Table 2 presents a listing of those agencies that have an inspections or similar function.

One might ask what types of inspections the OIGs are performing and how they differ from more traditional program evaluations conducted by other parts of the agencies listed. Basically, OIG inspections staff conduct four types of evaluations within federal agencies:

1. *Compliance reviews:* Is the organization or program doing what it is required to do?

Table 2. Inspections Function of Federal Agencies

Have Inspections Function	Have Similar Function	Intend to Develop Inspections Function	Have No Inspections
Commerce	Education	Railroad Retirement Board	Agency for International Development
Defense	Labor		
Energy	Office of Personnel Management		Agriculture
General Services Administration			Environmental Protection Agency
Health and Human Services	Veterans Administration		Federal Emergency Management Agency
Justice			
State			Housing and Urban Development
United States Information Agency			Interior
			National Aeronautics and Space Administration
			Nuclear Regulatory Commission
			Small Business Administration
			Transportation
			Treasury

2. *Efficiency and effectiveness studies:* How well and at what cost is the organization or program doing what is required?

3. *Policy analysis studies:* Should the organization's or program's legislation, regulations, or policies be changed?

4. *Snapshot studies:* What does the organization or program look like in actual operation?

Some OIGs conduct all four types of studies, while others concentrate on one kind. For example, HHS inspections staff carry out any of the four types depending on the issue, whereas General Services Administration (GSA) inspections staff primarily conduct compliance reviews.

Regarding ways that inspections differ from more traditional program evaluations conducted by other parts of the agencies, three features stand out:

1. *Short time frames.* The vast majority of inspections are short-term and do not usually include longitudinal studies that would scientifically follow a group of beneficiaries or organizational units over a number of years. For example, the evaluators in the Public Health Service follow heart patients over many years, collecting a variety of health data. OIG evaluators spend four months determining the efficacy of public cholesterol screening, in response to current issues being discussed by policymakers.

2. *In-house evaluators.* Inspections are almost always conducted by OIG staff, with contractors being utilized rarely for discrete portions of a study. Many traditional program evaluations are contracted out to consulting firms or universities, with the agency evaluators providing oversight and direction. Inspections staff employ contractors only for technical advice and assistance, while conducting the inspection themselves. Thus, a consultant may provide expert advice on a particular subject matter or advise on the use of a certain type of data collection instrument, but inspections staff conduct the actual discussion with the study respondent. This practice not only cuts down on length of time frames and on costs but also allows for better control of the study design, data collection, and analysis. It is also effective when minor modifications are necessary during the course of the study.

3. *Independent publication of findings.* The results of an inspection are not subject to higher-level editing within the agency. While traditional program evaluators may have to submit their results for review through the agency's chain of command, inspections staff know that their IG has the final say on the report that they publish. This does not mean that inspections results are not circulated for review outside OIGs for comment. What it does mean is that an IG can promulgate a report without concurrence from any other source within his or her agency. This authority becomes extremely important when dealing with sensitive or controversial subjects.

Despite these important differences, the fact remains that OIGs are carrying out program evaluations of various kinds within several federal agencies. And when one analyzes where the policymakers increasingly look for answers, it becomes clear that OIGs are a major source of evaluative data. Whether it is Congress asking about the effectiveness of Department of Defense procurement systems, OMB seeking cost-saving suggestions on the operation of foreign posts, or an agency secretary wanting the facts about the impact of rural hospital closures, the IGs are increasingly being consulted.

In reviewing the semi-annual reports that OIGs submit to Congress, and in examining the origins of the Reagan and Bush administrations' legislative proposals, it is clear that OIGs have, during the past ten years, become a major force in overseeing the executive branch. OIGs have identified billions of dollars in cost-savings, and the Congress and executive branch have enacted hundreds of legislative and regulatory recommendations based on OIG inspections reports. Audits and investigations have also had impressive achievements.

As a tool in the oversight function, inspections are increasingly used by policymakers in both the executive and legislative branches. The number of congressional and agency requests for studies appears to go up each year. Contrasted with the reduced role of more traditional program evaluation in federal agencies (see U.S. General Accounting Office, 1988), it seems reasonable to suggest that the responsibility for evaluating federal programs is increasingly shifting to OIGs.

Variety of Inspections Activities

To understand the methods that inspections staff use to conduct their studies, we should first look at some characteristics of those agencies that conduct inspections. Relevant data, gathered in late 1989, are summarized in Table 3. As indicated, eight federal OIGs currently conduct inspections within their offices. Each of these inspections staffs studies full-time the programs, policies, or organizational units of their respective agency. While some of these inspections resemble audits (for example, those in the GSA), a majority of the inspections would look familiar to more traditional program evaluators.

Regarding the location of the inspections function, six of the eight OIGs have created or are in the process of creating distinct organizational units for this activity. These units vary considerably in size, partially reflecting the overall size of their agencies. The Commerce unit is the smallest with 12 inspections staff members, while Defense employs more than 170 personnel in its inspections unit. The remaining two OIGs (GSA and State) lodge their inspections activities within the audit or investigations units.

Also, some agencies are highly centralized in their operations, while others are highly decentralized with most personnel located in their regional offices. Defense used to have inspections staff in various field locations as well as in Washington, D.C. However, they now have all their personnel in their Washington headquarters. HHS, on the other hand, has the vast majority of their inspections staff spread out across the country in eight regional offices, where roughly 100 of their 145 staff members reside.

Regarding staff qualifications, the two largest inspections offices (Defense and HHS) primarily employ program analysts, which is the federal classification used for program evaluators. And while GSA staff are primarily auditors, the head of the inspections staff is a program analyst. Energy uses general investigators and general engineers due to some of the individual cases they evaluate and the technical nature of their inquiries. Yet, a

Table 3. Inspections Characteristics

Federal Agency	Organizational Location	Staff Qualifications	Inspection Scope	Standards
Health and Human Services	Office of Evaluation and Inspections	Program analysts	Mostly systemic, a few targeted	OEI inspections standards (used evaluation, audit, and PCIE standards in developing own standards)
Energy	Office of Inspections and Analysis	General investigators and general engineers	Mostly targeted, some systemic	Government auditing, PCIE standards, I&A policy
Commerce	Office of Planning Evaluation and Inspections	Auditors, accountants, economists	Mostly targeted, occasionally systemic	Government auditing standards, Inspections manual
General Services Administration	Office of Audit	Primarily auditors	90 percent targeted	Government auditing standards, GSA procedures
Defense	Office of Inspections	Multidisciplinary teams (military and civilian), program analysts	Both targeted and systemic	PCIE standards, Inspections procedures
State	Office of Investigations, Office of Security Oversight	Multidisciplinary teams (Foreign Service officers and civilians), program generalists	Mostly systemic program inspections, mostly targeted postinspections	Government auditing standards, State Department procedures
United States Information Agency	Office of Inspections, coordination with Office of Audit	Foreign Service officers, auditors, or management analysts	Some systemic, more targeted in domestic inspections	Government auditing standards, PCIE standards, OMB directives
Justice	Separate inspections unit being established in OIG			

Note: GSA = General Services Administration, I&A = Office of Inspections and Analysis, OEI = Office of Inspections and Analysis, OEI = Office of Evaluation and Inspections, OIG = Office of Inspector General, OMB = Office of Management and Budget, PCIE = President's Council on Integrity and Efficiency.

review of the different types of work they perform reveals that they too function very similarly to program analysts.

Commerce, State, and the United States Information Agency (USIA) use a variety of disciplines. In fact, while some agencies use one classification more than others, a variety of disciplines can be found in most agencies, and several agencies utilize inspection teams that are deliberately multidisciplinary.

Regarding inspection scope, we noted previously that inspections may include compliance reviews, efficiency and effectiveness studies, policy analysis, and descriptive snapshots of a given organization or issue. Table 3 categorizes these different types of inspections into *targeted* looks at narrowly focused policies, issues, or organizations versus *systemic* looks at broadly defined issues or programs. One OIG (HHS) conducts mostly systemic inspections, three other OIGs (State, Defense, and USIA) conduct a mix of both, and the remaining three OIGs conduct mostly targeted inspections (data were not available for Justice).

Not coincidently, OIGs that conduct systemic inspections primarily employ program analysts, while the more narrowly focused inspections utilize the skills of auditors and investigators who tend to be more focused in their work.

In terms of standards utilized to ensure high-quality work, the government auditing standards have, in the past, been utilized by several agencies. This is mostly due to the close relationship between audits and inspections, both in terms of organizational proximity and prior training of staff. The President's Council on Integrity and Efficiency (PCIE), which is composed of all the Inspectors General and chaired by the federal Office of Management and Budget (OMB), has also published general standards for OIGs (President's Council, 1986).

In addition, a PCIE committee has drafted a set of standards solely for inspections activities, thus reflecting an inherent difference between an audit and an inspection. These PCIE standards are based on standards that the HHS OIG had already developed for their inspections work. The HHS standards were partially based on the two sets of standards endorsed by the American Evaluation Association, that is, the HHS standards used a process-oriented approach for the bulk of the content.

In addition to these broad traits summarized in Table 3, the various inspections units also share *short time frames* (two to six months). This is one of the most important traits of inspections. The purpose of this quick turnaround is to ensure that the questions from managers and policymakers are given timely responses.

Inspections staff also seem to employ a common outlook or attitude. It is probably best described as client-driven and results-oriented. In many ways, this attitude, as well as inspections work itself, is similar to that of Management Advisory Services (MAS), the fastest growing parts of the large accounting firms in this country. The MAS function provides management consulting advice on a wide array of economy, efficiency, and effectiveness issues for both private and public entities. It also is very client-oriented and depends on its results for future business.

Common Lessons from Inspections

Realizing that inspections differ across various federal agencies, but also recognizing that there are some common characteristics, what can we learn from the inspections conducted over the past ten years? The following six "tricks of the trade" may not be entirely new to some evaluators. However, for the federal evaluation community, these practices probably represent a departure from standard operating procedure.

Inspection Lesson #1: *Know what your client wants.* Knowing your audience before you start and being clear about the information needed will help greatly in focusing your design and crafting your recommendations. An early meeting with the primary client and continuous contact throughout the study have proved to be effective strategies for fulfilling client needs. If the client is somewhat uncertain at the beginning about what is needed, discussion of the draft design may help to determine the precise issues to be addressed.

Inspection Lesson #2: *Be flexible in your methodology.* Depending on the time available, the type of data required, and the budget, there may well be several ways to conduct any given study. Inspection methods run the gamut from computer matches, statistical analyses, and random-sample case reviews to purposive sampling of individual documents and personal interviews. The trick is to have staff skilled in diverse methodologies and knowledgeable about when to use each method.

Inspection Lesson #3: *Produce the report in time to be useful.* More than once, clients have said that if a report is not produced by a certain date, it will be of no use. If a congressional hearing is scheduled, a regulation due to be published, a secretarial briefing planned, a top-level task force meeting set, it does little good to provide information after those events have occurred. Decisions will have been made and events moved forward, regardless of the data from the study. On the other hand, if the report is on time, there is the opportunity for it to be used. And, if the report is useful, decision makers may ask for other studies in the future.

Inspection Lesson #4: *Produce short, readable reports.* Whether reports are for internal or external consumption, the more concise and focused the document, the more likely that managers and policymakers will read it. And, with advances in computer technology, there are many options for producing documents that say a lot with a few well-chosen graphics. Several inspections offices also use short executive summaries for high-level policymakers, while focusing the remainder of the report for low-level staff.

Inspection Lesson #5: *Make recommendations and track their outcomes.* Most inspections offices make recommendations and assess their consequences. If an inspection uncovers a problem during the study, a possible solution is offered. This proposed solution may not be the perfect answer, but it gives the responsible policymaker at least one option to consider. This recommendation also facilitates dialogue that could eventually result in even better answers.

Inspection Lesson #6: *Position yourself for objectivity.* The inspections function, as a part of an OIG, has one characteristic that may be difficult to replicate. Since Congress wanted OIGs to have the independence needed to be objective, the legislation establishing the various OIGs required them to report periodically to Congress, without going through their agencies' structures. This independence allows inspections staff to readily access information from a variety of sources within the agencies without being hindered or obstructed in reporting findings or making recommendations. Perhaps the lesson for other program evaluators is to position themselves so that they can objectively report findings in the broadest forum possible.

Questions About the Inspections Movement

This chapter suggests that program evaluation in federal agencies has changed over the past decade. First, there has been a change in attitude about traditional program evaluation, a diminution of program evaluation activity in many agencies, and the birth of a new evaluation function, inspections, in OIGs. Second, this relatively new OIG function contains some new methods, ideas, and attitudes for program evaluators.

However, whenever there is change, there is also a need to examine the effects of that change. A basic question is whether federal-level program evaluation is better off today than it was ten years ago. And, since we are particularly interested in the effects of inspections, to what extent has inspections played a role in the overall improvement or deterioration of program evaluation?

In asking these questions, we might divide them into two categories: First, how do the various types of program evaluation, including inspections, fit together *systemically* in any given agency? And second, has the *manner* in which inspections have been conducted contributed to or detracted from the betterment of program evaluation?

Systemic Questions. Does the current mix of program evaluation activities better meet the overall needs of federal-level agencies than did the mix that existed ten years ago? In looking at the different types of program evaluation (for example, program monitoring, short-term efficiency and effectiveness studies, and longitudinal impact studies) and at the various offices that conduct these studies (for example, operating components, the assistant secretary for Planning and Evaluation, and OIG), is there a better mix today?

Some might argue that federal program evaluation is healthier today because of the many changes that have taken place and the new mix that has developed. They might say that the traditional program evaluators are appropriately overseeing evaluation contracts that address basic research issues or important long-term solutions. These contracts may be for a multiyear period, which is necessary for gathering the data required for the questions asked. They might see that OIGs fill a much-needed evaluation role for short-term studies, as well as provide a more independent perspective in both asking questions and providing possible answers.

Others might argue just the opposite. They might feel that the traditional program evaluators have lost their ability to effectively carry out short-term studies and that they can no longer control the information flow to top-level policymakers. They may view the OIGs as interlopers in an area that belongs to traditional program evaluators rather than to offices that should be concerned more with fraud and abuse than with policy matters.

A second systemic question addresses the impact of each program evaluation unit and, more important, the sum of those impacts. In other words, in addition to a good organizational mix of evaluation activities, is each unit producing the type of results that are needed? Some might argue that the mix is good and that each unit, including inspections, delivers what is expected. Others might say that some, or even none, of the units is producing the type of information that managers and policymakers need.

A third systemic question is who, if anyone, should be coordinating the various program evaluations within an agency and how should coordination work on a daily, monthly, or yearly basis? For example, inspections products should not duplicate other evaluations already being performed. Some might suggest that if the various evaluative functions are allocated appropriately and if each unit produces its proper products, there may not be a need for overall coordination. Others might insist that, due to fluctuating priorities and the need to ease communications, this coordination role is essential in most agencies.

Conduct Questions. The first conduct question concerns the qualifications of those conducting inspections or other types of program evaluation. As we have noted earlier, individuals from different disciplines conduct inspections, including program and management analysts, auditors and accountants, and foreign service officers. Should only certain classifications be allowed to practice program evaluation, or are there certain skills that are prerequisites? Some might insist on specific, formal training, while others might want a combination of general training and specific skills or experience.

A second question about conducting inspections or program evaluations concerns the methods utilized. We found that inspections rely on a variety of different methods, depending on the circumstances. Some might ask if inspections methods are too client- and time-driven and wonder if the findings are valid. Others might say that using the best-known evaluation practices available for the time allowed to complete the project is a reasonable and sufficient way to proceed.

A third question concerns the standards that inspections use to ensure the quality of the work. While the PCIE has drafted a specific set of standards for federal inspections activities, should there be a common set of standards for all program evaluations? Some might argue that a common set of standards should apply to all persons engaged in program evaluation activities. Others might feel that as long as there are standards that meet an organization's needs and provide sound control over quality, then a variety of standards could meet program evaluators' needs.

Many other questions could, and should, be asked about inspections as a part of the world of program evaluation. As relatively young players in the evaluation world, there are several definitive questions that inspections staff might ask themselves. For example, should we consider ourselves evaluators rather than general policy analysts who happen to do evaluations? How should we define ourselves in relation to other evaluation overseers, such as the GAO? What kinds of skills should we stress when hiring new staff or training current staff? Should we think of ourselves as moving toward more traditional program evaluation or should we imagine ourselves more in the audit-related world of management advisory services?

This chapter was written to provide a sound, preliminary basis for reasoned and measured answers to some of these questions. The answers will be found through dialogue both within the inspections community itself and in the broader evaluation community. Perhaps some of the answers are provided in this volume.

References

President's Council on Integrity and Efficiency. *Quality Standards for Federal Offices of Inspector General.* Washington, D.C.: Government Printing Office, 1986.

U.S. Department of the Treasury. Office of Inspector General. *Agents for Preventing and Detecting Fraud and Waste.* Washington, D.C.: Government Printing Office, 1988.

U.S. General Accounting Office. *Program Evaluation Issues.* Washington, D.C.: Government Printing Office, 1988.

William C. Moran is the HHS regional inspector general, Office of Evaluation and Inspections, Chicago. During the period 1985–1990, he chaired an HHS OIG procedures committee that developed the procedures, standards, and methodology for the inspections function.

PART TWO

Case Studies of the Offices of Inspectors General

Rapid, responsive evaluation targeted to decision makers is increasingly becoming more important to improving the quality, efficiency, integrity, and cost of programs at the U.S. Department of Health and Human Services.

Evaluation Within the U.S. Department of Health and Human Services Office of Inspector General

Michael F. Mangano

This chapter tells the story of an effective evaluation unit within the U.S. Department of Health and Human Services (HHS). Inside the HHS Office of Inspector General (OIG), the Office of Evaluation and Inspections (OEI) has become increasingly important to department policymakers. At the same time, these OIG evaluators have also been testing new ways of doing evaluations. During the past five years, they have completed over 270 separate evaluations (often requested personally by top-level decision makers) and have reported back to top management using both short, snappy reports and personal briefings.

Our evaluations have helped improve services to the neediest of citizens, make those services more efficient, protect programs from possible fraud, and save billions of dollars in wasteful practices. Our studies have been reported in the *New York Times, Washington Post, Newsweek, New England Journal of Medicine*, NBC's "Today Show," and PBS's "MacNeil/Lehrer Newshour," all in the same year. And this is over and above the numerous times our evaluations have been quoted in trade publications such as *Health Policy Week, Modern Healthcare, Medicine and Health*, and *Health News Daily*.

We are also proud that public administrators have honored us twice. In 1987 the National Capital Area Chapter of the American Society for Public Administration gave us its annual Elmer B. Staats Award for Program Evaluation for our leadership in federal program evaluation. Also in 1987 the Public Employees Roundtable awarded us its prestigious Public Service Award for excellence in public service.

Another form of recognition is the number of groups asking our advice on how their own evaluations can be improved. In past years, cities (Boston, Las Vegas, San Francisco, Seattle), U.S. states (California, Massachusetts), Canadian provinces (British Columbia, Ontario), foreign countries (Denmark, India), and even nongovernmental organizations (League of Women Voters, fire departments, school districts, and hospitals) have all asked for our technical assistance.

Despite our success in Washington, D.C., however, we are practically unknown within the evaluation community, largely for two reasons. First, we work for the HHS Inspector General. When our findings are presented, they are presented as findings from the Inspector General, not from the Office of Evaluation and Inspections. This is as it should be, but it makes us less visible than other evaluation offices. Furthermore, the name Inspector General connotes more traditional audits or investigations, and many professional evaluators do not think of the Inspector General's office as a source of evaluations.

Second, our relatively low profile in the evaluation community is our own fault. We have been so busy *doing* evaluations that we have not spent enough time *telling* about them. We make too few efforts to publish in evaluation journals or to speak at evaluation conferences. While this is changing (for example, Thompson, 1989), we need to do more.

Origin and History of OEI

Our OEI has an interesting history. We were originally created because there was a gap in the HHS evaluation capability. At the cabinet and subcabinet levels in Washington, events move quickly, and decisions are needed just as quickly. Traditional evaluations are often too slow to help—in the past, decisions were regularly being made before the results of traditional evaluations were available.

Another problem is that traditional evaluations are not always targeted to focus on the exact issues facing decision makers. For example, none of the early evaluations of Head Start focused on developing a set of indicators for assessing the program's performance, even though at one time this was exactly what policymakers most wanted.

Joseph A. Califano, Jr., knew about this evaluation gap from his days in the White House as President Lyndon Johnson's domestic policy adviser. In the first days after President Jimmy Carter appointed him secretary of HHS (then Health, Education, and Welfare) in 1977, Califano decided that another evaluation mechanism was needed. So he quickly established an Office of Service Delivery Assessment (SDA) in the Office of Inspector General, and he instructed us to study only those issues that he or Hale Champion, his under secretary, personally requested. He also insisted that we report our findings back to him personally (Hendricks, 1981; Wholey, 1983).

For several years SDA activity successfully filled a gap in the department's evaluation capability, but the Inspector General eventually felt that SDAs were a somewhat limited tool. While SDAs were very timely and very much targeted on issues of interest, they also relied heavily on qualitative analysis from the local level. While this methodology was quite appropriate for many studies, the issues facing the department were changing, and the OIG needed a different methodology for new types of studies.

So, in 1982 Inspector General Richard P. Kusserow reshaped our methods into a new approach called program inspections (Kusserow, 1984, 1986). Our work remained timely and relevant, but we began to use more rigorous research tools to gather and analyze information (Mitchell and Hendricks, 1984-1985). For example, we began relying less on in-person interviews and more on record reviews, computerized extraction of existing data, and large-scale mailed surveys.

Today we have professional evaluators in ten different sites around the country. Our administrative offices, statistical analysts, and program specialists in public health, health care financing, human development, and social security issues are located in Washington, D.C., and Baltimore, Maryland. Most of our evaluations (called inspections), however, are not conducted by these experts at our headquarters but rather by our staff in regional offices in Boston, New York, Philadelphia, Atlanta, Chicago, Dallas, Kansas City, and San Francisco, totaling over one hundred professionals. In each of these regional offices we have fourteen staff members with considerable freedom and authority in conducting national inspections.

Topics Evaluated by OEI

One fascinating aspect of our office is the incredible diversity of the topics we study. The possibilities are almost limitless, mostly because HHS's responsibilities are so vast. HHS includes under its umbrella most of the federal human service programs, including social security payments, reimbursement for Medicare and Medicaid, direct health care from the Public Health Service, research conducted by the National Institutes of Health, and social services such as day care, Head Start, foster care, and adoption programs. The Inspector General has the authority to evaluate any of these areas.

In dollar terms, these programs cost a huge amount of money—$424 billion in fiscal year 1990. Few people realize that the HHS annual budget is the fourth largest in the entire world, trailing only the national budgets of the United States, the Soviet Union, and Japan. In effect, our office has the authority to evaluate, on a national basis, a set of activities roughly equal to the scope of the entire Canadian economy.

Not surprisingly, our workload is heavy and growing each year. We completed twenty-six program inspections in fiscal year 1985, a sizable accomplishment. By 1989, however, we had almost tripled our productivity to seventy-two inspections, and we fully expect to do even more in 1990. Our success has bred an increasing demand for our evaluations.

In addition to completing *more* evaluations each year, we also complete evaluations that are *more difficult*. For example, we use many different methods to gather data and the most sophisticated computer techniques to analyze those data. We also tackle socially sensitive issues such as hospital "dumping" of poor emergency-room patients, paternity establishment, adequacy of laboratory testing, and minority adoptions. And, not surprisingly, many of our studies are conducted under severe time pressures.

Methods for Conducting Program Inspections

Methodologically, our program inspections are a form of evaluation, but they also draw heavily from two other disciplines: policy analysis and operational auditing (Mangano and Rawdon, 1990). From evaluation we have drawn methods for designing instruments of sampling and data collection and analysis. From policy analysis we have drawn methods for focusing our inspections and communicating them effectively. And from operational auditing we have drawn methods for assessing the compliance and efficiency of services.

Perhaps even more telling, we take methodology seriously, and we devote considerable attention to ensuring that all our staff are highly skilled. We have recently developed a series of seven methodology manuals detailing the various steps of an inspection. These manuals cover how we focus the inspection, target the information needed, identify specific sources of information, gather information, analyze the information gathered, prepare an effective written report, and present an effective briefing.

In addition, all OEI staff attend regular training sessions to refresh their current skills and to stay up-to-date on new methods. In our most recent training (a four-day retreat) over one hundred OEI evaluators studied such topics as the design of effective discussion guides, graphics options, ethical use of statistics, strategies for increasing productivity with quality communications, and computer-assisted telephone interviewing techniques.

While each inspection is unique, almost all of them involve five discrete phases: pre-inspection, design, data collection, data analysis, and reporting.

Pre-Inspection. The first phase of any inspection focuses on what we will and will not evaluate. For this task we adhere to the following principles:

1. Focusing is a cooperative process that involves both evaluators and program managers, not a solitary activity of evaluators.
2. Focusing is a continuous process, usually involving an iterative approach and emergent designs.

3. It is important to begin with and keep an open perspective on the issues being evaluated.
4. It is important to consider seriously all reasonable options for conducting the inspection.
5. Because OEI exists to improve the department, every inspection must maximize the chances of yielding useful recommendations.
6. Because of all these requirements, it takes time to focus an inspection properly.

Following these guiding principles, we then (1) determine our primary and secondary audiences, (2) clarify the exact purpose of the inspection, (3) understand the activities to be evaluated, (4) understand the context of the inspection topic, (5) clarify the OIG role, and (6) establish the specific scope for the inspection. We do this by reviewing relevant documents, examining readily available data sources, meeting with a variety of relevant persons, and visiting local sites of the activities to be evaluated.

Design. After pre-inspection, we construct a formal study plan specifying our proposed approach, including purpose and objectives, background to the topic, specific issues and questions to be addressed, plans for data collection, plans for data analysis, expected products, staffing, schedule, and budget. In order to ensure that all involved parties have the same expectations for our inspection, we widely circulate this design and personally discuss it with key actors.

Data Collection. Because each inspection is uniquely tailored to the needs of its audience, the issues being evaluated, and the data available, we collect the necessary data in whatever ways make the most sense for each inspection. Generally this involves one or more of the following methods:

Computerized Extraction of Data from Existing Data Bases. For example, we were concerned that the Social Security Administration (SSA) was still paying benefits to decedents. In addition, we were also concerned that SSA lacked an effective mechanism to recover overpayments of this sort. By analyzing SSA's Master Beneficiary Records, we showed that SSA had paid almost $150 million to over 308,000 dead persons between 1978 and 1986. As a result of our findings, SSA took steps both to recover the misspent $150 million and to prevent such erroneous payments in the future.

Document Reviews of Written Materials, Tape Recordings, Films, or Videotapes. For example, even though HHS nonprofit grantees are encouraged to deposit their federal and grantee monies in interest-bearing accounts and to use the accrued interest to provide additional services, we were concerned that some grantees were not taking advantage of this opportunity. So we examined actual bank statements from 569 nonprofit grantees. We found that 80 percent of them were earning no interest on their bank funds, thus losing $4.25 million in interest from federal funds and $8 million in interest from grantee funds. Based on our evaluation, HHS issued new regulations requiring nonprofit grantees to deposit their federal funds in interest-bearing accounts, automatically creating an additional $12.25 million for direct services.

Record Reviews of Individual-Level Records or Files. For example, the department wants to ensure that as many children as possible benefit from the available Head Start slots. Federal regulations once allowed Head Start centers to enroll only as many children as there were seats in the classroom, and we were concerned that normal absences were creating empty seats that could be used to extend the service to other children. So we visited Head Start centers across the country and painstakingly reviewed enrollment and attendance records for 6,208 different class-months. We found that due to illness or other reasons, 18 percent of all Head Start seats were empty on any given day. As a result, HHS changed the regulations to allow Head Start centers to "overbook" a few extra children, and Head Start began overnight serving an additional thirteen thousand children at no additional cost.

Interviews with Persons Involved in or Informed About the Issues. Even though we gather hard data in several ways, almost every inspection also involves discussions with key persons. For example, we once wanted to learn more about the weaknesses of the federal computer systems in order to correct any vulnerabilities. So we visited several federal prisons and interviewed felons who had been convicted of violating those computer systems for their own personal gain. Even after allowing for the sources' self-interest, we learned that many of the same weaknesses in the systems still existed, and we were able to recommend better safeguards for the future. In addition to one-to-one in-person interviews, we also use group interviews (including focus groups), telephone interviews (including the latest computer-assisted telephone interviewing technology), and public hearings or community forums. Often these interviews suggest the need for additional data, which we then collect in order to corroborate and extend our interviews.

Mailed Surveys to Carefully Selected Recipients. For example, we recently wanted to determine whether SSA beneficiaries were satisfied with the services they received. SSA officials had made several changes in the program, and they planned even more changes. So it was important to gauge the effects. We mailed a structured questionnaire to a random sample of carefully selected SSA beneficiaries and tabulated the responses. Because our survey contained several questions asked on an earlier General Accounting Office (GAO) survey, we were able to compare satisfaction levels over time. As a result, SSA has been able to tailor new services to the ways beneficiaries prefer. This had led to an increase in telephone contacts in place of more time-consuming office visits.

Personal Observations by OEI Evaluators. For example, our inspection of senior citizen centers focused on events inside the centers, but we noticed a surprising number of expensive cars parked outside. While senior center programs are available without regard to income, our observations did raise the issue of whether it is appropriate for federal funds to provide free lunches for relatively wealthy senior citizens. Most of our observations are transient, but we have also used the three other types of observation: participant observations, observing participation of others, and surveillance.

Special Tests or Demonstrations of Systems or Procedures Being Evaluated. For example, we once wanted to ensure that runaway youths were, in fact, able to use the federally funded Runaway Youth Hotline to contact their parents if they so wished. Rather than review statistics or interview program staff and runaways, we tested the hotline directly by posing as runaways and calling the hotline from various locations around the country and at various times during the day. The results were shocking: It took an average of seventeen calls simply to reach a hotline operator; the first sixteen calls were either not answered or rang busy. Faced with these findings, the HHS secretary took immediate action and improved the program by increasing the number of available telephone lines and operators.

Data Analysis. In OEI, we pay special attention to analysis. For example, we believe that (1) each analysis is unique, with very few "rules" that hold true for every analysis, (2) analysis occurs throughout an inspection, not just at the end, (3) as an evolving, dynamic process, analysis may change focus as the inspection progresses, (4) nonetheless, it is still essential to develop an initial analysis plan while designing the inspection, (5) to persuade top policymakers, the analyses should be as simple and direct as possible, and (6) because it is so important, analysis should not be rushed.

We stress that interpretation of findings is ideally a collaborative process between program officials and our evaluators. Accordingly, we pay considerable attention to displaying preliminary findings so we can discuss them candidly with the officials involved.

Reporting. We directly report our findings and recommendations to top policymakers and program officials in two different ways, as detailed later here: short written reports and personal briefings.

Quality Control

Throughout each of these five phases of an inspection, quality control is uppermost in our minds. Because our credibility depends largely on the accuracy of our past evaluations, we simply cannot afford to report inaccurate findings or to offer recommendations that miss their marks. If we were to fail on either task, our findings and recommendations would quickly lose credibility in policy discussions, no matter how well we targeted our studies or how quickly we completed our work.

Accordingly, we ensure the quality of our inspections in three separate ways. First, we have developed a rigorous set of standards for our program inspections, some of which we borrowed from the two sets of standards endorsed by the American Evaluation Association, from the GAO's Standards for Audit of Governmental Organizations, Programs, Activities, and Functions (the famous "Yellow Book"), and from the President's Council on Integrity and Efficiency (PCIE). The PCIE is essentially *the* round table of all Inspectors General from twenty-four federal agencies, and the PCIE has established its own standards for OIG activities.

Second, all of our findings are documented in systematic work papers, which are compiled through the course of an inspection and filed at the end. These work papers allow us to tie each finding and conclusion back to the original, supporting data sources.

Third, all draft inspection reports are reviewed by our headquarters specialists, who are experts in the various HHS programs. These specialists pay particular attention to the policy and operational interpretations and implications of the findings and recommendations of each study. They also ensure that each report is internally consistent, can support its conclusions, offers only recommendations that directly follow from the findings, and is understandable to the intended audiences.

Products of Program Inspections

As mentioned earlier, we report our results in two main ways. First, we prepare written reports of our findings and recommendations, which we have learned to write for executives, not for researchers. The reports are short (fifteen pages, and always with an executive summary), appealing (we have desktop publishing capabilities, and we use graphics effectively), and balanced (we always present unbiased findings, and we include comments from program officials at the back of our reports).

Our reports are then distributed widely to relevant persons within the department, including the secretary of HHS, heads of major HHS components, program managers, and key staff, and to Congress, the Office of Management and Budget (OMB), and any other interested organizations outside the department. In the past, we have found our reports quoted at length in trade newsletters, speeches, and Congressional testimony, and even on the floor of Congress.

Second, we often conduct personal briefings for top HHS policymakers and program managers. Evaluation findings are often better conveyed in person than in writing, so we have spent considerable effort refining our techniques of presentation (Hendricks, 1982). We try to limit these briefings, which usually take about one hour, to a small and select audience so that we can create a forum for an active discussion of the issues.

A third type of inspection product is formal publication in various journals. As mentioned earlier, we publish too few articles in evaluation journals, but we do publish in other journals. In the past ten years, for example, results of our evaluations have appeared in numerous journals: *American Behavioral Scientist, American Journal of Epidemiology, The Bureaucrat, The Internist, Investigator's Journal, Journal of the American Medical Association, Journal of Clinical Research and Drug Development, Journal of Policy Analysis and Management, New England Journal of Medicine, Public Administration Review, Social Service Review,* and many others.

Outcomes of Program Inspections

Conducting over seventy evaluations per year and reporting our findings and recommendations to top-level HHS policymakers are satisfying tasks, but these accomplishments alone do not make us an effective evaluation office. What makes us effective is that circumstances *change* as a result of our evaluations. Our work improves the department and its services in at least four different ways.

First, we *improve the quality of services* provided by the department and its grantees. Based on our recommendations, the Health Care Financing Administration (HCFA) developed regulations that will improve the quality of skilled medical care provided to patients by home health aides. Our review of home health agencies had found a low level of training and supervision of aides. The new regulations mandated stricter supervisory controls and increased training requirements. In this case the changes came via regulatory changes, but at other times we stimulate operational improvements or changes in federal legislation.

Second, we *make services more efficient.* In our study of the Medicare program we found that hospitals were inappropriately billing Medicare as the primary payer for elderly victims of automobile accidents. The law requires automobile, liability, or no-fault insurers to pay first. In many instances, however, Medicare paid the claims as primary and made no attempt to recover payment. The HCFA agreed to implement the recommendations we made to improve procedures to identify hospital claims with accident diagnoses and determine whether Medicare was the secondary payer.

Third, we *identify vulnerabilities to fraud.* In conducting a study of the Aid to Families with Dependent Children (AFDC) program, we found an innovative way to prevent fraud at the pre-eligibility stage. We recommended that states institute a pre-eligibility fraud prevention program combining the eligibility workers' experience and intuition with the investigators' skills to identify and weed out false information. The Congress agreed with our approach and required this pre-eligibility fraud detection program as a condition of state plan approval. As another example, our inspection of Social Security cards was able to identify and correct ways in which individuals were fraudulently obtaining HHS services.

Fourth, and by no means least significant, we *save money* for the taxpayers. In the last five years we have recommended actions, implemented by Congress and HHS, that have saved over $5.8 billion, money that otherwise would have been wasted. In 1989 alone we saved the taxpayers $1.5 billion by showing, for example, how to save $570 million through improvements in child support enforcement, $230 million through reductions of fraud in the Aid to Families with Dependent Children (AFDC) program, and $150 million through detection of social security payments to decedents. In other words, we saved over $11 million dollars for each person on our staff, or over $200 for every dollar we spent running our office.

Reasons for Our Effectiveness

What allows our OEI to have such a positive impact on HHS? We believe that our success is due largely to six factors, which we hope can be duplicated elsewhere.

First, we choose our evaluation topics carefully. We only conduct studies that are targeted to specific topics of current interest and thus have a good chance of being influential. Currently, over one-third of our inspections are requested directly by the secretary, heads of major HHS operating divisions, OMB, or Congress. Our entire work plan, however, remains as flexible as possible in order to move quickly when a new opportunity becomes available.

Second, we have the variety of tools necessary to conduct effective evaluations. Perhaps most important, we have full legal authority to do our evaluations as we see fit. This involves both statutory and administrative authority, which allows us to gain access to and obtain data as needed. In fact, we have the authority to subpoena data if need be. We also have the technological resources we need. Our staff members—all 140 of them—are equipped with personal computers and have easy access to a wealth of other hardware such as fax machines, plotters, modems, headphones, and input scanners. We also have the software needed for word processing, data analysis, and graphics construction. WordPerfect 5.0, Lotus 1-2-3, PC SAS, Freelance, Chartmaster, Graphics Writer, Picture Perfect, Sideways, and Banner are but a few of the more than thirty different software programs available in OEI.

Third, we have high-quality staff. No evaluation office is better than its staff, especially one that conducts almost all of its work in-house, as we do. We recruit actively, and we have recently hired outstanding scholars from such prestigious universities as Cornell, Harvard, Stanford, UCLA, University of London, and Yale. We are especially proud of the diversity of skills that our staff bring to our evaluations. Currently, we have evaluators, attorneys, journalists, statisticians, computer programmers, physicians, and sociologists on our staff.

In addition, we take training seriously: All employees have individual training plans that are updated each year. Our training policy requires a minimum of eighty hours of formal training for each employee every two years, with at least one activity each year. Last year alone 135 OEI staff took a total of 321 training courses, and this does not count the more informal, and perhaps more valuable, on-the-job experiences.

Also, we have an annual week-long training workshop for all staff in all offices. This year we will conduct intensive training, for each regional office, on our new series of methodology manuals. To complement this training, we believe in close supervision by experienced evaluators.

Fourth, we emphasize timeliness. We recognize completely that if evaluations are to be useful, they must be available before decisions are made. We aim to complete each inspection within four to six months, and we are sometimes much faster. This year, for example, we conducted for the secretary an inspection on hospitals that were closing, and we completed the work in only four weeks.

Fifth, we believe in active promotion of our findings and recommendations. We recognize that the ultimate product of an evaluation is information, but we also know that information is only effective when it reaches the proper audiences. Accordingly, we do not wait for others to seek us out; we aggressively look for opportunities to tell what we have found, what it means, and what should be done as a result. Furthermore, we do not forget our recommendations once we offer them. We track their status, especially those accepted, to ensure they are implemented as agreed.

Sixth, we have a unique independence within HHS. While we are certainly a part of the department and have access to all department information, we also have a separate responsibility outside the department. In the legislation creating the OIGs, Congress mandated that OIGs would report to two masters: their respective secretaries and Congress.

Although the Inspector General works for the HHS secretary and reports to him or her, at the same time the Inspector General also reports completely independently to Congress. Because of this dual status, we in OEI have the best of both worlds. We have the "insider" knowledge of the department and its workings, yet we also have the "outsider" independence to act as we judge best.

Trade-Offs

The evaluation niche we fill at HHS emphasizes short-term studies of current topical interest to decision makers. While we believe this approach has been successful, we also realize we are making trade-offs in the process. We are not, for example, conducting many long-term impact or comparison-group studies, which are important for future policy developments. By concentrating on topics of immediate importance, we are forgoing some of long-term importance. While we believe our methods of conducting rapidly paced analyses are sound, the time factor can affect the methods we choose and how we apply them. And we want to be influential so we place great importance on meeting the needs of decision makers. But this latter decision also has implications. We assume decision makers know what they need or ask the right questions, which is not always the case, so we must be careful.

In sum, we recognize the trade-offs we are making. We believe we fill an important evaluation niche. At the same time we understand the need for other types of evaluations and admire those who perform them. We recognize that we have more to learn about evaluation and about how to conduct our evaluations even more effectively.

References

Hendricks, M. "Service Delivery Assessment: Qualitative Evaluations at the Cabinet Level." In N. L. Smith (ed.), *Federal Efforts to Develop New Evaluation Methods.* New Directions for Program Evaluation, no. 12. San Francisco: Jossey-Bass, 1981. Reprinted in E. R. House (ed.), *Evaluation Studies Review Annual.* Newbury Park, Calif.: Sage, 1982.

Hendricks, M. "Oral Policy Briefings." In N. L. Smith (ed.), *Communication Strategies in Evaluation.* Newbury Park, Calif.: Sage, 1982.

Kusserow, R. P. "Program Inspections." *Government Accountants Journal,* 1984, *33* (1), 1-6.

Kusserow, R. P. "Program Inspections: A New Form of Rapid Evaluation." Paper presented at Peat Marwick/Royal Institute of Public Administration Conference on Policy Management and Policy Assessment, London, England, February 1986.

Mangano, M. F., and Rawdon, B. "Issuing Reports Not Covered by Auditing Standards: What Are They? What Is Required?" *Government Accountants Journal,* 1990, *39* (2), 49-53.

Mitchell, B., and Hendricks, M. "New Program Evaluation Tools." *Bureaucrat,* 1984–1985, *13* (4), 39-41.

Thompson, P. "The (Evaluation) Role of the Office of Inspector General." *Evaluation Practice,* 1989, *10* (3), 43-44.

Wholey, J. S. "Service Delivery Assessment: A Goal-Free Evaluation Process." In J. S. Wholey (ed.), *Evaluation and Effective Public Management.* Boston: Little, Brown, 1983.

Michael F. Mangano is the deputy inspector general, Office of Evaluation and Inspections, Office of Inspector General, U.S. Department of Health and Human Services. During the period 1985–1990, he has overseen the production of over 350 evaluation studies, given numerous interviews to radio, television, and print media, and regularly testified before Congress.

Quick, unannounced management evaluations by the U.S.
Department of Commerce Office of Inspector General are helping
that department improve its efficiency and effectiveness.

The Inspections Program Within
the U.S. Department of Commerce

Charlie Hall, Johnnie Frazier

The U.S. Department of Commerce has been likened to Noah's ark—the difference being that the ark had two of everything whereas Commerce has only one of everything. Commerce satellites probe the earth's atmosphere, its ships map the ocean floor, and its planes plot the course of hurricanes. Its agencies make direct and guaranteed loans, count the U.S. population, promote and control trade, recommend telecommunications policy, finance public radio and television facilities, and regularly assess and report on the status of the nation's economy. Commerce agencies also run the nation's patent and trademark systems, manage the research necessary to establish U.S. standards and benchmarks, lead the country's minority-business development efforts, and perform a wide range of other functions crucial to the country's well-being.

The department's diversity is further reflected in the locations and number of its organizational units. Altogether, Commerce has some five hundred major headquarters units, eight hundred field locations throughout the United States and in sixty-five foreign countries, and thousands of grant and loan recipients. All need periodic audits and independent evaluations to better ensure that their goals, objectives, and missions are being carried out in an efficient, economical, and effective manner.

The requirement for periodic audits and evaluations was significantly strengthened by one sweeping law: the Inspector General Act of 1978 (Public Law 95-452). With this act Congress mandated that Commerce and most other federal agencies establish Offices of Inspectors General (OIGs). OIGs were charged with, among other things, performing the audits, investigations, and evaluations that they deem appropriate. After making these reviews, OIGs are to (1) develop and present their findings, conclusions, and recommendations, (2) ensure that appropriate measures are taken to correct the problems found, and (3) report the results of their reviews to a variety of senior government officials, including Congress.

Despite the impressive mandate, by early 1982 we recognized that about 97 percent of the Commerce Department's numerous headquarters operations, field offices, contractors, grantees, programs, and other operations had never been audited, evaluated, or even visited by an OIG audit staff. With projected resources, 97 percent would remain unaudited at the end of the next five years. The impossibility of performing traditional audits on all these operations and programs led the Inspector General (IG) to look for a creative solution. The result was the establishment of the Commerce OIG inspections program.

Traditionally, OIGs have relied on comprehensive audits to evaluate the efficiency and effectiveness of their agencies' programs and operations. Management audits review a program or an activity to determine whether (1) it is being carried out in compliance with applicable laws, regulations, and sound accounting procedures, (2) its resources are being managed efficiently and economically, (3) adequate internal controls are in place, and (4) the intended benefits are being realized.

But the requirements for conducting these audits are fairly rigid—they must follow the generally accepted government auditing standards, or GAGAs—and take many months and staff hours. Few, if any, OIGs have the resources to undertake the number of audits they consider ideal or warranted. Inspections are an effective way to bridge the gap between the ideal and the real.

Simply described, inspections are minimanagement audits, quick program surveys, or short-term evaluations. They give special agency managers timely information about current operations and problems. Their recommendations encourage managers to use available resources more effectively, efficiently, and economically.

The Inspections Function Within the Department

As might be expected, the objectives of an inspection parallel those of a management audit but also provide a great deal more flexibility to the evaluators. At Commerce, inspections have been instrumental in improving government services in several key areas:

1. *Evaluation of the efficiency and effectiveness of the office, program, or activity inspected.* During 1987 and 1988 we issued two inspections reports recommending that the Minority Business Development Agency (MBDA) close two of its district offices, one in Boston and one in Miami. We had concluded that MBDA could maintain program effectiveness, improve staff

utilization, and reduce operating costs by closing the two offices. The MBDA director responded by asking us to inspect the offices in Philadelphia and Los Angeles and assess the effectiveness of the overall district office structure. We agreed to do so. The additional inspections and our evaluation of the regional offices' staffing and workload requirements led us to conclude that the four district offices should be closed. Closure of the district offices would result in better utilization of the regional staff and a reduction in operating costs.

2. *Identification of major systemic program or management problems that need close study in the form of detailed management audits.* While preparing for an inspection of one of ninety-six weather-observing stations, we learned that the National Weather Service (NWS) has used balloon-borne instrument packages called "radiosondes" for more than fifty years to gather data on the vertical and horizontal distributions of pressure, temperature, and humidity. Ground-based tracking systems compute changes in the radiosondes' positions to provide winds-aloft data in addition to the three upper-air measurements. These readings, together with surface, satellite, and radar observations, provide the three-dimensional pictures of the atmosphere needed to forecast weather.

In 1980 the National Oceanic and Atmospheric Administration (NOAA) began a program to test the feasibility of the "wind profiler," an automated upper-air measuring device. Further research is needed, but a five-year demonstration network of thirty wind profilers is planned for fiscal years 1988–1992. If the demonstration is successful, a national network might be proposed, with deployment to begin about fiscal year 2000.

However, our inspection revealed that the current equipment was not expected to last until the new technology could be developed. Further complicating the matter, two vendors who were awarded contracts to supply radiosondes had been unable to obtain approval of specific contract requirements. This was delaying production and delivery schedules. Meanwhile, NWS's ninety-six observation stations were using about sixty thousand radiosondes each year and the supply was dwindling. We referred our observations and concerns to the OIG Office of Automated Information Systems for a more thorough review of the situation. In the interim, we recommended that NWS work with its parent agency, NOAA, to develop a contingency plan to ensure that the supply of radiosondes would not be affected by nonconformance of radiosonde contractors.

3. *Detection of possible wrongdoing that should be investigated.* Thefts from imprest funds, misuse of government funds, and conflicts of interest are a few of the problems disclosed by inspections and referred to the OIG Office of Investigations, where the matters were developed and pursued as potential criminal cases.

4. *Establishment of a strong IG presence to generate the critical intangible*

of deterrence to fraud, waste, and abuse. This factor is well illustrated by our inspection of some of NOAA's meteorological observatories. NSW maintains forty-seven of these observatories to gather data from surface, upper-air, and radar measurements. The data are sent to other NWS offices where they are used in preparing forecasts and warnings. The observatories also alert NWS to potential or imminent severe weather, but they provide little or no direct public weather services. Twenty-eight of the observatories are run by private contractors; the others are staffed by NWS employees.

We inspected the observatories at Seattle and Quillayute, Washington; Portland, Maine; and Chatham, Massachusetts. Most responsibilities were being handled effectively in spite of recognized inefficiencies. For example, the equipment used to take upper-air observations was antiquated, and spare parts were limited. A labor-intensive method of collecting surface observations is scheduled for automation by the end of 1994. The new system should reduce observation time by more than two-thirds and allow a redirection of staff to other services. Our inspections also revealed that both the Seattle and Quillayute observatories had been run by contractors for several years, saving the government substantial amounts of money. Before our inspections, the observatories had not received any independent audits or evaluations. Word quickly spread that OIG was inspecting the observatories and that special efforts should be made to make sure that *all* were in good shape.

Organizational Structure and Staffing

The Commerce inspections function is located within the office of the assistant inspector general for Inspections and Resource Management. As of March 1990, the inspections staff included twelve people: the program director, who is also a deputy assistant inspector general, ten full-time inspectors, and a secretary. The headquarters-based inspections staff encompasses a wide range of degrees and backgrounds in industrial engineering, accounting, business administration, economics, auditing, and criminal investigation. Inspections teams are routinely supplemented by individuals from other Commerce OIG units in Washington, D.C., as well as by staff personnel from OIG regional offices with computer science, procurement, legal, and other backgrounds. We also call on outside experts with specialties not available within OIG.

The level of experience also ranges widely, from individuals well versed in Commerce programs to entry-level personnel. We are excited that our current inspections staff now includes three recent college graduates. Like the other individuals whom we routinely enlist for short-term assignments from other parts of OIG, these new recruits bring fresh ideas and enthusiasm to the program.

What to Inspect?

With an enormous scope of possibilities to consider, we put a great deal of time and effort into selecting the inspections we will perform each year. The IG has final authority to approve selections for the annual work plan. However, the inspections staff and all other Commerce OIG units, especially the Office of Audit, assist in identifying and recommending candidates for inspection. They do this based on their own knowledge, plans, and experience. We also solicit ideas and recommendations from the department's top managers, key program personnel, and heads of operating units. Finally, we consider the audits and evaluations planned for the year by the General Accounting Office (GAO).

Since inspections are intended to narrow the gap between our audit needs and resource realities, as discussed earlier, an essential factor in selecting inspections targets is OIG's annual audit plan. Once it is clear where the audits will be conducted, we are in a better position to plan our work to complement them. We can plan our inspections in areas that have not been audited, or are not scheduled for audit. We can also use inspections to spread OIG coverage more evenly throughout the department's many separate agencies. For example, if the auditors have not scheduled a review at the National Institute of Standards and Technology, we would try to schedule one or more inspections there.

Knowing what to inspect is very important. Obviously, everything does not lend itself to an inspection. We would not, for example, normally attempt to use an inspection to evaluate the overall effectiveness of a large program function such as that of NWS. Nor would we be likely to inspect the operation of one of the department's major accounting systems. Instead, we would inspect a particular aspect of the weather program: how selected aspects are functioning or how the program is operating at a particular site.

Since most inspections are intended to be unannounced visits (a crucial aspect of the inspections process discussed in detail later here), the official annual plan is presented to the public in general terms only. For example, it may state that four inspections will be made of an agency's field offices, but it will not name the offices. The actual sites, which may not be determined until several weeks before the inspection, are selected after getting information from several sources. We survey recent OIG and GAO audit reports that have identified areas requiring further study, analyze requests from departmental officials who suspect program fraud or mismanagement, and review past annual plans to ensure that we include sites never visited before. Hence, the plan is a working document that is designed with flexibility. This flexibility is one of the keystones of our inspections program. It enables us to respond quickly to unforeseen needs and requirements. We know from experience that between 25 and 40 percent of our inspections each year will be determined by special requests and circumstances. The annual plan—in fact, the entire inspections program—must anticipate last-minute changes.

The Inspections Process

An inspection usually takes about fifty staff days. A team of two to four inspectors spends about a week to prepare, a week making the actual on-site inspection, and about a month briefing agency officials and preparing a written report. Within days of the team's return to headquarters, the IG and then top officials of the inspected agency are briefed on the findings. Within weeks after the actual on-site inspection and briefings, a draft report is prepared and submitted to the director of the inspections program for review. Once the director's review is complete, the draft report goes through an internal OIG quality-assurance process.

It is helpful here to talk through the inspections process in some detail.

Once the inspections target has been chosen, a team is put together by the director of the inspections program and a team leader designated. To the maximum extent possible, the team includes individuals who have expertise relevant to the unit being inspected. If, for example, we are inspecting a unit whose primary functions depend on automated systems, we will include on the team an individual with extensive automated data processing (ADP) expertise. We did this in a recent inspection of the computer-oriented operations of the Bureau of the Census. We made sure that a computer "ace" was on our team so that we would be on equal footing with the experts we would surely encounter. Similarly, we know the importance of having a contract negotiator on our team when we inspect any of Commerce's many contractors.

An effective team leader is crucial to the success of any inspection, since the leader must plan and direct the work, mold the team into a coordinated group, make rapid decisions, and communicate effectively. Team members are expected to have a good grasp of the assigned subject matter, be able to analyze and present conclusions quickly, and demonstrate professionalism, objectivity, and independence in getting the job done.

Being prepared is an absolute must for every inspection. The team members prepare themselves by thoroughly reviewing pertinent information about the activity to be evaluated, including its mission, goals, budget, staffing, reports, and a variety of other relevant data available to OIG. The team leader prepares a plan stating the purpose and objectives of the inspection, including any special matters to be reviewed.

Most domestic inspections are unannounced, so no advance warning is given. With the arrival of the inspection team at the site, we simultaneously inform a predetermined headquarters agency-liaison person that an inspection is underway. In some cases, such as when the organization to be inspected is outside the continental United States, it is impractical and sometimes even impossible to make unannounced visits. In those cases, we notify the organization in advance.

The inspection begins with an opening conference, during which the team leader briefs the senior program official on the objectives and general scope of the review, introduces the team members, and arranges for work to begin. The actual work includes the following activities:

1. *Interviews with employees of the inspected activity.* These are essential to an inspection's success. No one knows better than the employees what is really going on. Another, more practical reason for heavy reliance on qualitative data from interviews is the length of the on-site visit. Although time constraints often do not permit detailed or extensive examination of records, it is important that our reviews involve all levels of the unit. So while we select those we need to interview, we offer everyone an opportunity to meet with us at any time or location—anonymously, if desired. On many occasions we have uncovered serious management problems during interviews conducted after working hours in our hotel rooms, with individuals who wanted to remain anonymous. With assurances and guarantees of confidentiality, people are more willing to reveal instances of fraud, waste, and abuse. This has led, for example, to employees providing sufficient leads and information for the inspectors to uncover unethical actions by supervisors, illegal acts by managers, and abuses of authority by others. We often develop questionnaires or interview sheets to facilitate and expedite the interviews. These are designed to ensure that essential information is gathered and to encourage candid and broad discussion of the issues.

2. *Interviews with clients, beneficiaries, and users of services provided by the activity inspected.* These might include, for example, the U.S. businesspersons who depend on International Trade Administration employees to help them export goods and services overseas, or the many organizations and people who depend on NOAA weather forecasts. Most important, interviews are a fast way to find out from an informed source what is really happening at a facility. As with the employee interviews, these can involve the use of questionnaires, with guarantees of anonymity.

3. *Physical surveys of the inspected program or operations coupled with the inspectors' personal observations.* Personal impressions are crucial to the inspections process. For example, during our inspection of a major supply center within NOAA, our inspectors discovered that gaps in the chain-link fence surrounding the facility would allow unauthorized entry, sign-in registers were not used properly during nonbusiness hours, windows were not reinforced, and employees carrying large packages could exit the center without having the packages checked by security personnel. These observations—which resulted from examining the site very carefully, not from studying departmental regulations—led to meaningful recommendations to

improve the center's management and security. After all, inspectors are paid to think and offer opinions based on informed judgments.

4. *Examination of pertinent documents and records.* By examining relevant documents, taking photographs of conditions we find, and otherwise gathering evidence, we are able to support our observations and conclusions. Defensible evidence ensures broad acceptance of our inspections results.

Once the team completes its on-site work, the team leader arranges a briefing (a closing conference) for the official in charge in order to discuss the preliminary findings. Within a week, the team briefs appropriate headquarters officials. Candid discussion of inspections results with these officials helps ensure that the findings are factual and the conclusions and recommendations are sound and reasonable. These briefings are a fundamental and critical component of the inspections process.

Before briefing the senior agency officials, however, the inspections team goes through a series of internal OIG debriefings. The team meets with the assistant inspector general and the inspection program director to organize and refine the results of the inspection. Pertinent aspects of the observations and conclusions are discussed and validated with OIG legal staff and other relevant OIG personnel. In fact, as part of the quality-assurance process, appropriate management audit officials review the first drafts of our inspections reports.

As soon as the team leader and the inspections managers are satisfied with the positions, strategies, and recommendations, they all enter "the lion's den"—more commonly known as the IG's office. The IG in Commerce has made clear that he expects a lot from the inspectors in a short time. The briefing with the IG, his deputy, and his special assistant is conducted in a defensive atmosphere with the IG and his immediate staff playing the role of devil's advocate. Are these sessions usually grueling? Yes! Are they informative and helpful? Always! Loose ends and any areas in which the team is unprepared quickly surface. These sessions make the team's subsequent encounters and briefings with agency officials a relative breeze.

The Inspections Report

Within thirty days of completing the inspection, the team prepares a draft report on the results, including recommendations for correcting any problems. The assistant inspector general sends the draft report for review and comment to appropriate officials of the involved departmental office or operating unit. Those officials must return their written comments within thirty calendar days.

The reactions of reviewing officials are a critical part of the inspections process. The officials are encouraged to be candid and to indicate, for each finding or recommendation they accept, the corrective actions they have taken or propose to take. For each finding or recommendation they reject, they must state their reasons for disagreement.

The IG signs and issues the final report within thirty days of receiving the written comments. The final report includes findings and recommendations, addresses the agency comments, discusses opposing views, and includes a copy of the written comments. If the written comments are not received within the required thirty days and a time extension is not granted, the IG may issue the final report without comment.

Frequently, an inspection unearths a major problem that requires extensive additional review and analysis. When this occurs, the problem is referred to the appropriate OIG unit (either the Office of Audits or the Office of Investigations) for action. For example, MBDA awarded a large grant to a minority contractors association. Our surprise inspection disclosed major deficiencies, both financial and administrative, in the management of the grant funds during the twenty-four-month grant period. The deficiencies included (1) unexplained cash transactions that did not appear to benefit or relate to the grant award: eighty-four checks drawn to cash, totaling $72,915, could not be traced to supporting documentation, (2) taxes not paid on time: payroll taxes were not withheld and deposited monthly as required, and (3) significant expenses charged to the grant that should be disallowed or questioned. We recommended that MBDA stop funding the association until the problems raised by the inspection were resolved. We also recommended a comprehensive financial audit, which eventually confirmed our observations.

In another inspection we found major program weaknesses that warranted the attention of top department officials. But this inspection also revealed that the head of the inspected entity had used government funds to make personal purchases at Saks Fifth Avenue and Bloomingdales. We turned this over to the OIG Office of Investigations. The ensuing investigation led to the criminal prosecution of this individual.

What Makes the Inspections Process Work?

We believe that our inspections program, tailored to the particular needs of our OIG and the Department of Commerce, has been extraordinarily effective. This view has been reinforced by the significant results generated and the enormous support given to the program by senior officials of the agencies we inspect. These results have included (1) significant dollar savings, (2) commitments from managers to use their resources more efficiently, (3) strengthening of internal controls, (4) revamping of entire programs, (5) identification of wasteful practices, and (6) correction of many policies, practices, and procedures that were found to be contrary to the government's best interests.

We find that our success hinges on five indispensable factors: First and foremost, the program works because of its people, the inspectors. In creating the inspections program, we recognized that we would need good people with diverse abilities and talents. The inspectors' collective array of backgrounds provides insight and perspective that would not be possible if all had the same background, for example, auditing or management analysis. Further, the inclusion of young individuals direct from college campuses keeps everyone's perspective fresh. By offering salary levels that are slightly higher than average and providing more-than-usual authority and flexibility, as well as an assortment of other incentives, we made the inspectors an elite group. The members have consistently remained with the program as others have persistently sought to join it. The interest in this program demonstrated by so many OIG staff members has made it easy to include people from all parts of the office on inspections teams. Usually the short-term team members bring with them a great deal of enthusiasm and make valuable contributions to the inspections effort.

Second, the inspections program has flourished because of its access to up-to-date information on Commerce programs and activities. The adage that "information is power" is true. The inspectors rely on having good information in (1) selecting the units and activities to be inspected, (2) planning the inspections, (3) conducting the inspections, and (4) monitoring the targeted agencies' efforts to address inspections findings and recommendations.

With the assistance of an excellent OIG information specialist, the inspectors are able to obtain comprehensive data on almost every aspect of Commerce operations. The Inspector General Act of 1978 helps in this regard, since it guarantees OIG access to all departmental records and files. We are privileged to use the vast majority of the department's automated data bases and can extract information on just about any facet of its business. We can see, for example, the budget deliberations and approved budgets for all of the department's programs, people, and operations. We also know which projects are being proposed by Commerce managers and which are recommended for elimination. We can also monitor departmental awards of contracts, grants, and licenses. We have continued access to data on areas the department considers vulnerable to fraud, waste, and abuse. These data sources give us a definite advantage in determining where our inspections efforts can best be applied.

The information in Commerce systems is supplemented by the information we routinely obtain from department officials, managers, and personnel. The inspectors must know what is going on throughout the department. Hence, they work closely with the other OIG managers and auditors who specialize in specific Commerce programs and functions in order to remain up-to-date on changes. They have also developed and maintain working relationships with many of the department's key managers and officials. In fact, we assign individual inspectors a number of agencies and officials with whom to maintain liaisons. These contacts provide invaluable sources of information.

Third, there is the unannounced nature of our work. The lack of advance warning provides an intangible—but very real—deterrence factor. If managers never know when OIG will visit, they are more likely "to walk the straight and narrow." But unexpected visits provide another benefit as well. We see operations as they really are, not spruced up to impress an OIG inspections team. This enables us to get a more realistic picture of a unit's operation.

On occasion, the unit head or primary manager is not there when we make our visit. This enables us to see how the unit functions on its own. Some of our personnel were initially skeptical of the unannounced approach, but it has given our inspections a unique and beneficial perspective.

Surprise inspections, of course, can cause managers to be overly defensive and even annoyed. But this has *not* been a problem. Department managers (1) have been well informed (warned) that they can be inspected at any time, (2) are aware from the Inspector General Act that it is OIG's prerogative and responsibility to conduct its work as it sees fit, and (3) view an inspection of their operation as simply their turn and the luck of the draw. Moreover, we carefully select as team leaders those individuals who have the ability to defuse explosive situations and calm anxious managers. Again, the importance of the personnel factor is seen.

Fourth, our success depends on our ability to respond quickly. Inspections are designed for quick reaction to the needs of OIG and of the senior officials of the agencies we inspect. The IG frequently uses an inspection for a quick assessment of unforeseen or questionable management issues and even of potential wrongdoing. Inspections have often been conducted to assess allegations of management problems and charges of wrongdoing that arrive via OIG's confidential hotline. Senior agency officials sometimes ask for an inspection of a particular unit because they see or suspect a problem and want help. Such was the case when we were asked to look into allegations of financial improprieties at a Commerce trade center in Mexico City. When any problem needs quick and objective assessment, with reliable feedback and reporting, an inspection is an excellent response.

The last essential component of our program is the inspectors' access to the very top decision makers in the agencies we inspect. For example, when we inspect one of the hundreds of offices of NWS, we brief the assistant administrator of NWS as well as mid-level officials on the results. Because of the similarities of many field offices, he is likely to distribute our report to those other offices with the implied message that they had better not have these same problems. Hence, the inspection message spreads rapidly.

Although in the beginning there was some doubt that we could attract and maintain the interest of these senior officials, we have found that they tend to appreciate independent assessments of their field offices' function-ing. Too often, their knowledge of what is happening in district offices has been filtered through layers of management. They fear that what they know is what someone down the line wants them to know, which is not neces-sarily the truth. Another factor is that often the problems encountered at one field location are systemic and exist at others. And finally, our inspec-tions briefings advise senior managers of the positive things we find. This is welcome information.

Historically, evaluators—especially auditors and OIG personnel— "audit by exception." This usually translates to concentration on negative observations. Too often, the sole measure of many evaluators' work is the number of problems and negative findings they uncover. Clearly, our pri-mary objective is to identify problems needing attention. But as we evaluate the many programs within the Department of Commerce, we see many accomplishments and efficient organizations and practices. We enjoy high-lighting such findings in our reports. Ironically, we usually must work harder to support and document positive findings. As a rule, it takes only one or two graphic examples to show that problems exist, but much more is needed to convince supervisors that programs and organizations are working well.

While we provide inspected units with written reports, our briefings with top agency officials often include additional material that is better conveyed through frank oral discussion. This includes matters and con-cerns that were not sufficiently developed to include in the written reports, but that still warrant management's attention. Managers see these discus-sions as very helpful and recognize that the inspectors are more interested in correcting problems than in writing voluminous reports.

Charlie Hall is the assistant inspector general for Inspections and Resource Man-agement, Office of Inspector General, U.S. Department of Commerce. He was instrumental in creating the Commerce inspection program and served as its first director.

Johnnie Frazier is the deputy assistant inspector general for the Office of Inspec-tions and Resource Management, Office of Inspector General, U.S. Department of Commerce. He serves as the program director for the inspections program.

The Inspector General has done a great deal to further management improvement efforts in the Department of Defense, utilizing inspections as one major tool in that effort.

Inspections Program Evaluation Within the U.S. Department of Defense Office of Inspector General

William F. Vance

Before and since the Inspector General Act of 1978, a number of studies, both public and private, identified problems of management in the Department of Defense. Mollenhoff's (1967) study enlightens us about the character of Defense officials involved in controversies and scandals. And, as recently as last year, the Ill Winds criminal investigation into illegal activities designed to influence Defense procurement decisions gave the department and a few of its contractors scandalous notoriety (U.S. Department of Defense, 1988-1989).

Will the Inspector General office be the ultimate congressional fix to what Colson (1989, p. 9) calls a crisis of character "where men and women trade character for cash and sacrifice commitment on the altar of selfishness"? Probably not, but the Inspector General function does create the force to expand internal management control, as well as to heighten organizational and programmatic oversight.

One way the Defense Inspector General has enhanced the capability for management oversight and internal control has been the inspections program evaluation function created in 1982. This chapter explains the history, operation, and impact of this relatively new activity.

Evolution and Organization

The Inspector General Act of 1978 (Public Law 95-452) created a number of presidentially appointed Inspectors General to (1) conduct and supervise audits and investigations relating to programs and operations of federal entities, (2) provide leadership and coordination and recommend policies for activities designed to promote economy, efficiency, and effectiveness of programs and operations, and to prevent and detect fraud and abuse, and (3) provide a means for keeping the heads of federal entities and the Congress fully and currently informed about problems and deficiencies relating to such programs and operations and the need for and progress of corrective action.

The Inspector General for Defense was established in 1982 by an amendment to the Inspector General Act of 1978. The inspections activity is not specifically identified in the law as a distinct function of federal Inspectors General, as are audits and criminal investigations, but the extensive mandate that Congress gave the Inspectors General requires a flexible and broadly defined approach. That is why the inspections function of the Defense Inspector General is designed to assess organizational and programmatic effectiveness, compliance with public law and departmental policy, and prevention and detection of fraud, waste, and mismanagement.

Other types of Defense program evaluations (including various types of operations research, audits, and investigations) are quite narrowly focused. Audits must conform to audit standards of the U.S. Comptroller General, so auditors are often compelled to limit the scope of their reviews and to develop detailed data to support their findings and conclusions. Investigations must be conducted in accordance with accepted law enforcement investigative procedures.

Inspections, in contrast, have been designed to provide in-depth analyses across broad organizational and functional areas. As a result, any given inspection can cover a wide range of subjects. For example, the inspection of Defense management of wholesale fuels covered the management process; acquisition of facilities, services, equipment, and products; storage and distribution of fuels; and wartime readiness. Also, the inspection of the Defense Mapping Agency was designed to assess the mission success of the agency, particularly its effectiveness in managing requirements for mapping, charting, and geodetic (MC&G) products (prioritization, dedicating resources to produce the products); production and modernization planning (MC&G production planning and modernization of production equipment); distribution of MC&G products; resource and information management (ADP systems integration and management); and physical, information, and communications security.

The current Defense inspections staff has evolved from the Inspector General element of the Defense Logistics Agency. It is located near the Pentagon in Arlington, Virginia, and now has a staff of 178 professionals: 147 civilians and 31 military officers skilled in various disciplines needed to evaluate programs and joint organizational operations. These professionals are organized into (1) staff units to plan and develop inspections policy and procedures and to analyze inspections processes and (2) five line divisions to execute and report results of planned inspections. The professional skills available in the line divisions include specialists in budget and financial systems, communications, personnel, contracting and procurement, computer science, health systems, logistics management, supply management, quality assurance, transportation management, industrial systems, and program and management analysis. Any additional skills needed for any particular inspection are provided from resources available within the Defense Inspector General organization or from elsewhere in the department.

Types of Inspections

Inspectors General within each branch of the military services originate in separate provisions of law, and they inspect activities within their respective service branches without assistance or oversight from the central departmental Inspector General. Each of these Inspectors General reports to the Secretary of the respective military department. Their inspections focus primarily on military operational readiness and matters related to esprit de corps. This focus supports the field commanders and complements, rather than duplicates, the inspections work of the Defense Inspector General, who reports directly to both the Secretary of Defense and the Congress. The Defense Inspector General conducts three different types of inspections: organizational, functional, and verification.

Organizational inspections evaluate the efficiency and effectiveness of joint organizational activities that are chartered independently of a military service such as the Defense Logistics Agency or the Defense Intelligence Agency. Organizational inspections focus on the essential processes that these joint activities depend on to achieve their missions, including the functions and management of all their internal organizational elements. The inspection of the Defense Intelligence Agency, for example, examined the agency's work structure and the effectiveness and efficiency of its internal controls and management operations in procurement, automated data processing (ADP), security, personnel, budgeting, and logistics.

Functional inspections evaluate the Defense programs, or subject areas common to all Defense components, that provide services or support to the entire Defense community. The review of hazardous material and hazardous waste management, for example, analyzed Defense policy and its implementation throughout the department. This functional inspections effort included site visits to seventy-two Defense installations or field commands in the continental United States and overseas. The problems in managing hazardous material and hazardous waste were so severe that a long-term Defense Inspector General strategy evolved to address specific environmental problem areas for departmental decision makers. Functional inspections like this examine the processes of the specific function as well as the effects on the various Defense components (including the military departments and defense agencies) and on non-Defense activities of private-sector contractors or of other federal departments and agencies. Other examples of functional inspections are the evaluations of family and child care services for Defense personnel, information resource management, commercial passenger airlift operations, and security policies and practices in the department.

Verification inspections are undertaken only after an organizational or functional inspection has been completed. These inspections determine whether the appropriate officials have taken corrective action on previously identified problems or have implemented recommended changes in management procedures. These inspections also determine whether the corrective actions have been completed and are effective and efficient. An example is the verification inspection of the Armed Forces Institute of Pathology, a follow-up of an earlier organizational inspection of the Institute.

The Inspector General had inspected the Institute in fiscal year 1985 and had documented eighty-eight problem areas. The verification inspection evaluated the adequacy of actions taken to address these problems and found that 70 percent of the previous findings were valid and the related recommendations should have produced the intended results. The *significant* findings remaining open after this verification work included the need for improving laboratory methods for the Armed Forces; revision and enforcement of regulations for submission of case material; the need for Department of Defense policy for charging fees for civilian consultation services; insufficient jurisdictional authority for autopsies; safety problems associated with the precious metal recovery program; the need for improving the cost effectiveness and utility of the Armed Forces Medical Museum located at the Walter Reed Army Medical Center in Washington, D.C.; funding for additional building space for the Center for Advanced Education; and the lack of an active internal control program at the Institute.

Inspection Topics

The range of potential inspections topics (organizational and functional) is broad and includes joint activities among Defense agencies: manpower, reserve affairs, and personnel; international programs and security assistance; planning, research and development, intelligence, and space systems and programs; logistics, acquisition, and resources management; general administration; safety, environment, health, and medical; and comptrollership, budgeting, finance and accounting, and information resources management and automated information systems.

The specific topics come from diverse sources: Congress, Secretary of

Defense, Inspector General, military departments and Defense agencies, and internal improvement initiatives such as Cheney's (1989) Defense management report to the president. In addition to congressional requests, actions by an Inspector General can be mandated by law. The Defense Fiscal Year 1990 Authorization Act, for example, requires the Defense Inspector General to inspect the U.S. Soldiers' and Airmen's Home, a community facility located in Washington, D.C., for retired military personnel. Inspections of the Defense Intelligence and National Security agencies are examples of internally developed topics that cover joint activities by Defense agencies. Subjects are researched and prioritized based on the needs and requirements of the organization or program, visibility to the Department of Defense, and cost impact on the Department of Defense and ultimately on the taxpayer. And before topics are approved by the Inspector General, the anticipated results of the inspection must be of demonstrable value to the department and to national security.

Planning: The Key to Effectiveness

Effective planning provides the depth and scope for defining specific inspections goals and objectives. Essential to the planning function is an analysis of the requirements for a successful inspection and a strategy for undertaking it. Inspections planning focuses on the performance of an organization's or program's mission to assess its efficiency and effectiveness. Planning data on the inspections topic, collected and analyzed prior to on-site inspection, (1) identify the reasons why the organization, or program, is being evaluated, (2) identify the product or mission of the organization or program, (3) summarize the results of all previous evaluations (for example, inspections, studies, audits, reviews, congressional hearings, and General Accounting Office coverage) and their impact on the new evaluation, (4) give an overview and details on the universe of the organization's or program's operational world (interaction with or service to or from other organizations or programs such as the Defense Mapping Agency, the State Department, and many private-sector users), (5) identify oversight mechanisms and internal controls as well as how the organization effects such program controls, (6) identify management or special interest issues, (7) outline the criteria for determining or measuring an organization's or program's performance (for example, timeliness, quality, and quantity), and (8) provide goals and objectives for the evaluation based on knowledge gained in the planning process.

The entire planning process requires frequent and extensive travel by our plans analysts to Defense operations, customers, and suppliers throughout the world. Data gathered and analyzed by planners are provided through interviews, examinations of records, and automated data bases and management information systems.

Essential Elements of Information

Critical to any successful inspections program evaluation are Casey's (1974) Essential Elements of Information (EEI). These include the expertise and tools of operational procedures needed by the inspections team, as well as the knowledge gained by detailed planning and inspector training for the inspections topic. In addition to the EEI, extensive coordination within the office of the Inspector General, the Defense Department, and external organizations (such as the General Accounting Office and oversight committees of the Congress or other federal departments and agencies) helps ensure that all relevant and available information is considered in defining the scope of the evaluation. Such coordination also helps avoid duplication of effort.

EEI give the inspectors insight and focus for analyzing the efficiency and effectiveness of programs and management efforts so that problem areas can be identified and recommendations developed for improvement. The basic EEI are brought together and presented to the inspections team in a comprehensive, integrated package called the "planning fact sheet."

For each fiscal year inspections program, planning fact sheets serve as baseline documents for preparing the inspections concept plan, a more refined and detailed EEI "blueprint" for each inspections evaluation effort. The planning fact sheet is not merely a single-page summary of the inspections topic but rather a detailed and comprehensive research document, some nearly twenty pages in length. The fact sheet describes the inspections topic and anticipated results as these relate to the Defense Department's mission and overall national security objectives. Further, the fact sheet explains the need for the inspection and concentrates on systemic, or substantive, problems that potentially inhibit the organization or program to be evaluated from effectively and efficiently providing goods or services to the department. Succinctly descriptive, but comprehensive in nature, inspections planning fact sheets (1) describe the scope of the inspection and identify its specific objectives, (2) identify major issues that should be addressed, (3) project the resources needed (personnel, time, and cost), (4) identify potential inspections sites based on statistical sampling techniques, (5) identify the inspector skills and need for specific technical experts (for example, nuclear weapons specialists or MDs), and (6) determine the inspections goals, scope, and objectives as influenced by an analysis of the type of organization, program, or system and its impact on the Defense mission; applicable departmental policy, public law, and other federal rules or regulations; previous or ongoing audits, inspections, investigations, or other studies and reviews, either internal or external to the department; and information received from visits to policy and field operations, as well as from selected visits to customers.

Developing the Concept Plan

Beginning with the planning fact sheet, the inspections director develops a more detailed concept plan. This plan illustrates the targeted organization's or program's elements and actions that are critical to achieving a successful service or product. The concept plan also outlines the specific measurement criteria used to evaluate these essential factors. Such criteria include (1) validity or relevance of mission, service, or product, (2) quantity or timeliness, if applicable, (3) quality of product or service (for example, accuracy, completeness, clarity, and conformity to standards), and (4) product or service cost related to potential benefits, both quantitative and qualitative.

The interactive elements, or processes, of the organization or program should ensure that efficient and effective service or product support meets the needs of the customer. For example, our inspection of the Defense Personnel Support Center addressed, among other things, the requirements and procurement processes for supplying uniforms to the customer—in this case, the uniform services. These processes included product specifications, contracting, manufacturing, quality assurance, financial management, and transportation. They are interactive in nature and are evaluated individually as a function within a system, and collectively as a system (process). They are central to the inspections objectives of (1) substantiating the need for the organization, program, or system, and evaluating the effectiveness of the process of determining the requirements for the product or service, (2) assessing the organization's or program's policy for consistency, coordination, timeliness, and cost-effectiveness, (3) assessing program planning, budgeting, and execution for achieving objectives effectively and efficiently, and (4) determining whether organizational and functional oversight mechanisms for internal management control are working to identify and correct vulnerabilities and matériel weaknesses.

Inspections Methodology

The planning process produces the planning fact sheet and program information for the inspections team. The inspections director, assisted by a steering group that includes the plans analyst, then assimilates all available information and develops the inspections concept plan. After the plan is approved, the inspections team spends a predetermined period of time visiting the inspected activity and its organizational elements, customers, and policy proponents in the military departments or in the office of the Secretary of Defense. Planning visits vary in number of sites and time allotted, depending on the complexity of the inspections topic. For example, the inspection of the Defense Communications Agency included planning visits at a dozen locations.

As agents of the Inspector General, inspectors have unrestricted access to all official records and information within the Department of Defense. Only the Secretary of Defense may deny access, if he or she determines that such access will impair the national security. However, no Secretary of Defense since the enactment of the Inspector General Act of 1978 has ever exercised this authority.

With open access to information, the inspections team gathers and evaluates data on the inspected activity to identify problem areas needing increased management attention for improvement of program efficiency and effectiveness. Inspections program evaluations emphasize management improvements rather than compliance with policy, directives, regulations, and rules, although compliance issues are not ignored. Management improvements may be different work methods or organizations, use of a different product, or elimination of steps, procedures, or products.

Inspections teams range in number of inspectors from four to twenty or more, depending on the topic scope and complexity. Inspections teams are multidisciplinary in composition because various skills are needed to evaluate technical and other management and administrative areas. Most inspections teams are subdivided into smaller units to concentrate on specific subject areas. This division of labor gives the entire inspections effort a degree of flexibility to cover geographically distant locations within the time allocated.

Questions and identified problems relating to compliance with policy, absent of suspected criminal activity, are addressed in terms of the processes involved. Once inspections teams have gathered both quantitative and qualitative data, analysis is conducted in the context and framework of the approved concept plan. Depending on the specific subject matter, cost-benefit analyses are performed with a computer program specifically designed for this purpose. Recommendations to change policy direction or for departmental legislative initiatives may result. Inspectors look beyond strict compliance with regulations and look at how effectively the mission and related functional responsibilities are performed. Products, services, activities, and internal and external relationships are emphasized.

Inspections are interactive processes involving program managers in the organization or particular functional area inspected. Inspections findings, generically called "observations," are concise reports on situations that affect the mission of an organization or program. They are the principle data used by an inspections team to identify problem areas for the program manager. Unless there are unusual circumstances, such as severe time restrictions or indications of potential criminal activity, observations are written down, coordinated, and left with the program manager after each inspection. Varying in length and number, the reports generally are three to six pages long and range from thirty to one hundred or more observations for each inspection. They are structured to identify (1) *conditions* or the existing situations or deficiencies needing corrective action or improvement, (2) *causes* or the circumstances that produced the conditions or deficiencies, and (3) *effects* or the impact of the conditions or deficiencies on the organization or program. Effects are often quantifiable in terms of potential benefits, performance, and time, or they may be qualitative, such as the degradation of operational readiness or poor morale among personnel.

All observations include (1) applicable references to policy, regulation, or law, (2) discussion of the problem in relation to applicable references, (3) an impact statement that addresses quantitative or qualitative effects, and (4) recommendations for corrective action or management improvement. Observations are given to the responsible program manager for review and coordination to ensure that the facts are accurate. Questions concerning the facts as they are presented, or differences of opinion relating to the findings or conclusions, are discussed with the program manager by the inspections team. Corrective actions are suggested, but program managers are not obligated to follow them as long as their own corrective action fixes the problem.

Departmental procedures for disputed Inspector General findings ensure that decisions are made at each appropriate level for resolution. Program managers have the opportunity to disagree with findings when the draft report of the inspection is provided for comment. Continued disagreement will classify, or "flag," the findings for additional resolution. This process involves another unit of the Defense Inspector General organization, a unit that independently and objectively mediates the dispute through negotiation, if possible. If disagreements between the Inspector General and a Defense program manager are still unresolved after this mediation effort, the issue is elevated to the deputy secretary of Defense for a decision, though the resolution process rarely reaches this level.

Ensuring Evaluation Quality

Quality of the inspections product is enhanced by application of Total Quality Management principles and effective internal management controls during the life cycle of the inspections process. During each phase of the inspection, from planning to write-up of the final report, extensive in-process reviews are held to confirm that the right data have been collected and analyzed to support an assessment of each goal and objective. In-process reviews are both management and peer reviews. The time frame from the start of planning through publication of the report varies with the complexity of the inspections topic and type of inspection (organizational, functional, or verification). For organizational and functional inspections, it usually averages six to eight months. Verification inspections are much shorter and take less time.

An added element of quality assurance is the inspections steering group. It is formed to assist the inspections team as the inspection shifts from the planning phase to the execution phase. The steering group, under the leadership of the inspections director, is composed of the principal plans analyst, inspections team chiefs, and the inspections program director. Although this group is formed to help write the concept plan, it validates the basic planning data contained in the planning fact sheet.

To enhance continuity throughout the inspection, the plans analyst usually serves as the assistant inspections director. And, inspections program directors provide a quality-assurance dimension since they have different reporting channels. They provide not only technical advice to inspections teams but also independent and objective management oversight as "internal ombudsmen" and facilitators.

Inspections results reported to Defense managers and to Congress conform to quality standards set forth by the President's Council on Integrity and Efficiency (PCIE). Inspections results also follow internally adopted, inspections evaluation policy and procedures that greatly expand the PCIE standards. Before final reports are published and distributed within the Defense community, program managers are informed of the contents and are aware of all divergent views in advance. Published reports of each inspection are available to Congress and reports that are not restricted because of security considerations are available to the general public. (All Inspector General reports are listed in the Inspector General Semi-Annual Report to Congress.)

In addition to applying PCIE standards to Defense inspections management and operations, the Inspector General personally approves all inspections topics and periodically reviews and provides direction for the inspections executed. These reviews give each inspections director an opportunity to update the Inspector General on the progress of the inspection: what has been learned, the data gathered, and the information gaps that need to be filled for full assessment of inspections objectives. The Inspector General's personal guidance during program review updates can realign the inspections focus because of vital new information critical to the department and to national security. Other issues in need of examination are also identified during these reviews.

Lessons learned during individual inspections subject the entire inspections process to internal critiques by inspections directors, inspections program directors, inspections team chiefs, and individual inspectors. Improvement of inspections policies and procedures as well as refinements in analytical processes often result. Reports on lessons learned are required from inspections directors after each inspection. These are often complemented by comments and recommendations from the more energetic and ambitious inspectors. Verification inspections of previous work, in addition to confirming that corrective actions have been taken, also provide valuable insights for improving the quality of inspections methodology.

Inspections Results

Inspections program evaluations are not always warmly received by managers of Defense organizations and programs, but positive results for the department and for the taxpayer are net benefits. For example, an inspection of Defense management support activities (organizations that provide a depth of technical expertise to the office of the Secretary of Defense) revealed overstaffing. As a result of this inspection, two hundred positions were eliminated.

Another example is the inspection of the Merged Account. The Department of Defense is appropriated money by Congress to pay bills for all Defense programs, ranging from payrolls to weapon systems. These appropriations are made available for specific periods of time, after which any unused funds are merged, or transferred, into a Treasury account known as the "M" Account. For example, operations and maintenance funds are available for obligation for one year, and other appropriations, such as procurement funds, are available for longer periods of time. The "M" Account is the account into which unliquidated (unpaid) obligations are transferred after the appropriations have expired. Defense can still use the funds in this account, but only under certain conditions. The Defense portion of the "M" Account amounts to $12 billion, or 70 percent of the total funds available.

Inspection of the Merged Account, undertaken at the request of the PCIE, revealed serious systemic problems in the areas of reconciliation and validation, oversight, and policy. In addition, accounting data were found to be inadequate because of weak internal controls and poor record keeping. The results of this inspection have generated a great deal of congressional interest, and statutory changes have been introduced that will affect the department's policy covering the use of this account. Efforts are underway to improve the quality of the accounting data and to bring the department's accounting systems into full compliance with General Accounting Office standards. As these efforts progress, the degree of confidence in financial management data will continue to increase. Other federal departments and agencies with Merged and Surplus Accounts will be similarly affected.

Strengthening the Inspections Process

Certainly, not all Inspector General inspections in Defense are problem-free. Internal inspections procedures and analytical processes, for example, are examined during verification inspections. Problems identified and mistakes made in the past are addressed to prevent their repetition. The verification inspection of the Armed Forces Institute of Pathology, for example, yielded valuable insights about prior inspections results. The verification inspection confirmed that 70 percent of previous findings were valid and that their related recommendations should have achieved the desired results. The remaining Inspector General findings, however, had either been overtaken by events or were not sufficiently detailed for corrective action to be taken. The lack of sufficient details could have resulted from insufficient training or even an absence of the analytical framework needed to articulate the conditions, causes, and effects of the problems identified. Certainly, one lesson learned from this verification effort was that the methodology available to the inspections team to assess potential benefits was inadequate. Capitalizing on this insight, a methodology to analyze potential benefits has been developed. Verification inspections thus provide an internal inspection, quality-assurance function as well as an oversight mechanism for internal management control efforts in Defense.

Defense program managers, like other federal managers, often need proactive evaluation support on new initiatives. While Inspector General operational activity in the Defense community is not limited to audits and criminal investigations, inspections program evaluations are not clearly authorized by law. Existing inspections functions within the federal Inspectors General organizations represent an interpretation of the broad congressional mandate of the Inspector General Act of 1978.

Had inspections been included along with audits and investigations in the Inspector General Act of 1978, the law would have clearly recognized the role and importance of the inspections process to federal managers and would have provided a firm foundation for the inspections mission. It would have also fostered early development and adoption of uniform Inspectors General inspections policies, procedures, and standards. Inspections, as an effective program evaluation tool for managers, have become a distinct professional discipline.

Ambiguities relating to the responsibility of the Defense Inspector General in the realm of "inspections" haunt oversight of nonstatutory departmental Inspectors General. Nonstatutory Inspectors General have been established in some of the Defense agencies. These Inspectors General report directly, or indirectly, to the heads of their respective agencies and are assigned various roles and responsibilities and have different work methods and procedures. The degree of their autonomy within their agencies is subject to the authority of the agency heads.

Consistent inspections policy and procedures complementing application of uniform inspections standards by these nonstatutory Inspectors General organizations would enhance independence and objectivity and thus improve their agencies' management efficiency, effectiveness, and economy of operations. The Defense Inspector General inspections of the Defense Investigative Service and Defense Mapping Agency revealed that each agency Inspector General was unable to fully assess the agency's mission performance based on definitive and uniform Inspector General standards, including standards recommended by the PCIE. And, as a result, inefficiencies and ineffective management practices are perpetuated. If the Defense Inspector General had policy oversight of these nonstatutory Inspectors General, uniform policies, procedures, and standards could be implemented with positive results.

References

Casey, J. H. "Meeting Management's Information Needs." In R. M. Leighton (ed.), *Perspectives in Defense Management*. Washington, D.C.: Industrial College of the Armed Forces, 1974.

Cheney, D. *Defense Management Report to the President*. Washington, D.C.: Government Printing Office, 1989.

Colson, C. *Against the Night*. Ann Arbor, Mich.: Servant Publications, 1989.

Mollenhoff, C. *The Pentagon*. New York: Putnam, 1967.

U.S. Department of Defense. Office of Inspector General. *Semiannual Report to the Congress*. October 1, 1988—March 31, 1989, pp. 3-8.

William F. Vance is the director of Inspections Plans, Policy, and Analysis for the Inspector General, U.S. Department of Defense.

PART THREE

Questions and Concerns About Inspections by the Offices of Inspectors General

OIG activities are evaluative in some senses, but they cover a narrow set of potential evaluative criteria that are needed to judge the worth of social programs. If OIGs are becoming main players in program evaluation, a dangerous trend is developing.

Inspections as Program Evaluation: A Partial Overlap

David S. Cordray

For over a decade, staff within the Offices of the Inspectors General (OIGs) have been carrying out their oversight responsibilities with little public fanfare. Judging from the chapters in this volume, staff within these offices have been busy (they issue lots of reports), their products have been useful, and, given their growth (in number, staff size, and studies), they are likely to be a permanent part of the oversight landscape. Moran (this volume, p. 16) notes that "contrasted with the reduced role of more traditional program evaluation in federal agencies . . . , it seems reasonable to suggest that the responsibility for evaluating federal programs is increasingly shifting for evaluating federal programs is increasingly shifting to OIGs." He goes on to suggest that the addition of inspections has left the federal program evaluation enterprise healthier than it was ten years ago. If this is true, it seems reasonable to devote a volume of New Directions for Program Evaluation to describing the activities of some of the OIGs.

Still, we may want to step back for a moment and ask whether the nature and scope of the program evaluation field has been enhanced by this shift in emphasis. A positive response to this question might be to welcome these professionals as full-fledged program evaluators. After all, the program evaluation profession is eclectic and thrives on diversity of opinion, method, perspective, and disciplinary allegiance. Mangano (this volume, p. 25) highlights new ways of doing evaluations, and Moran suggests that learning would be reciprocal.

A less optimistic response would likely dismiss inspections as irrelevant to the evaluation enterprise, or worse, see it as diverting funds from the truly important types of studies that can provide meaningful answers about program effects, cost-effectiveness, and generalizability. A more balanced or cautious response—one that I articulate here—might be to look closely at some of the implications of equating or subsuming inspections under the label "program evaluation," or more generally, "evaluation."

Inspections Look Like Evaluation (Sometimes)

Each of the chapters in this volume provides a slightly different view of inspections and the role of OIGs. There are, however, some common themes that suggest a close tie with current and past program evaluation activities. These themes, no doubt, stem from the original charge for OIGs established in legislation. In part they also reflect changes in the U.S. information-gathering policy of the recent administrations. In adapting their procedures to meet their official charge and other changes, OIGs describe inspections in a way that resembles characterizations offered by other applied social researchers.

In describing the salient features of inspections, each of the other chapters in this volume highlights (1) the importance of understanding the needs of clients, (2) the production of relevant and timely information, (3) the importance of the planning process and the use of study designs as an empirical base for obtaining facts and making recommendations, (4) the need for flexibility or methodological diversity (that is, there are few standard procedures that can be uniformly applied), (5) the essential role of quality control in the overall product (that is, the inspector is held accountable to standards of proper conduct), (6) the value of independence from program management and the political pressures of top-level administrators, and (7) the need for succinct and effective communication. These are common features or characteristics that resemble program evaluations and policy analyses, and they are probably equally applicable to audits. At this level of discussion, inspections do not look much different from other forms of applied social research (broadly defined). But a close examination of what OIGs do, as opposed to how they do it, shows some important points of departure.

Inspections Focus on Selected Criteria

The Inspector General Act of 1978 (Public Law 95-452) created a number of independent OIGs along with a specific set of implied assessment criteria that would (1) promote the economy, efficiency, and effectiveness of federal operations and (2) prevent and detect fraud, waste, and mismanagement. It is not surprising that the examples presented in this volume focus on successes in these areas. And, while there is some overlap with the focus of traditional program evaluation, at least with respect to issues of program efficiency and cost-effectiveness, other aspects of OIG inspections (especially in the area of fraud) represent relatively uncharted domains for most traditional program evaluators.

Further, even where there are interconnections, the style of assessment is likely to be different for OIGs. For example, the idea of cost-effectiveness within the OIG perspective appears to focus on questions like "Could the government achieve greater savings from a program or activity by reorganizing the entity?" and "Can we achieve higher return on investment by requiring grantees to deposit funds in interest-bearing accounts?" Both of these suggested actions—the results of inspections—would achieve more cost-effective management of federal funds. These are not exactly the types of questions that program evaluators would ask or try to answer.

For example, under the auspices of cost-effectiveness, traditional program evaluators would focus on two quite different issues. First, the concept of effectiveness generally connotes some attempt to estimate, using experimental designs, the relative, quantitative difference between two or more treatment interventions. Second, by ascribing costs to each intervention, both monetary and nonmonetary (for example, lost opportunities), a judgment can be rendered about the value of achieving the observed differences. I am not suggesting that OIG emphasis on cost-savings is inferior. Rather, I am merely pointing out that the terms "effectiveness" and "cost-savings" connote quite different activities, methods, and perspectives for OIG inspectors than for program evaluators. Therefore, the common terminology between fields is somewhat misleading. Although it is the case that both types of assessment, regardless of how we label them, are important forms of governmental oversight, OIG-style inspections bring some new perspectives to the program evaluation enterprise.

Programs or Governmental Operations?

Collectively, OIGs have authority to inspect the operation of a vast number of federal entities that consume a major share of the federal budget. These entities include actual programs (those that provide services or transfers, directly or indirectly, to citizens or other recipients) and infrastructures within the government. The latter are generally the organizational vehicles by which programs are managed. Some are support services that are only indirectly connected with what evaluators think of as programs.

In looking over the examples of successful inspections provided in this volume, it appears that a great deal of OIG time is devoted to an examination of the infrastructure of programs and not to the full programs as we think of them. As such, the emphasis is different from that of program evaluation. To be sure, program operations depend on an efficient and effective governmental infrastructure; the point here is that inspections look at programs through a different, albeit complementary, lens. But if OIGs are increasingly becoming the source of program evaluations in the federal government, it is necessary to consider if theirs is the only lens through which we want to judge federal programs.

Status of Other Evaluative Perspectives

How should programs be judged? Whose perspective—managers, Congress, the public—should be used to judge programs? Is evidence on program efficiency or the absence of fraud sufficient to meet the needs of all stakeholders or to declare programs successful? On what criteria or set of criteria should we make our evaluative judgments? This set of questions goes to the root of recent concerns about the health and well-being of federal program evaluation efforts. As reported by Chelimsky, Cordray, and Datta (1989) and Cordray and Datta (in press), there have been serious and consistent reductions in program evaluation activities directed at assessing the effects or impact of government-sponsored innovations. In particular, the results of that research painted the following picture of nondefense program evaluation activities:

1. In 1980, 180 units in nondefense departments and agencies engaged in program evaluation activities; by 1984, 133 reported similar activities, representing a 26 percent decline since 1980.
2. Over this period, fiscal resources for program evaluations declined by 37 percent (in 1980 constant dollars), whereas agency budgets increased by 4 percent.
3. Resources for the most active evaluation units in 1980 declined by nearly 60 percent.
4. Staff assigned to the evaluation function declined by 22 percent, from about fifteen hundred in 1980 to twelve hundred in 1984.
5. Despite changes in staff and funds between 1980 and 1984, the number of evaluation studies decreased by only 3 percent.

As we noted (Chelimsky, Cordray, and Datta, 1989), the impression of greater efficiency—same or more work with fewer resources—is misleading. The same kind of work was not being done either in 1984 or 1988 as had been done in 1980. Information for internal program management won out over external information for Congress and the public. Between 1980 and 1984, reports were increasingly for internal consumption, produced at the request of program managers and disseminated primarily to them. Short-turnaround, management-oriented, internal, nontechnical reports replaced, in large measure, more complex evaluations that usually provided more precise measurement of program effects. When impact studies were conducted, increasingly they were the result of congressional set-asides. That is, in 1980, 40 percent of the studies were sponsored via congressional set-asides; by 1984, 60 percent of the resources came through set-asides. This pattern of staffing, funding, and types of studies suggested to us that program evaluation had declined to a dangerous level, and, when it was conducted, it was increasingly becoming a tool for internal management, not for public oversight. Response to this set of findings about the health and well-being of traditional program evaluation was mixed. Although some members of the evaluation profession mourned the decline, others celebrated the demise of the experimental tradition. For example, staff in the Office of Management and Budget argued that this trend was a step in a positive direction since, from their perspective, traditional program evaluations were not useful and should be replaced by small-scale studies that assisted government officials in managing their programs. The chapters in this volume present the same tone and perspective.

Such a harsh judgment wrongly condemns traditional, large-scale, effects-oriented evaluations. Recent evaluations have demonstrated that early criticism of the traditional program evaluation enterprise was somewhat premature and misguided. Although it is true that early effects-oriented studies, taken one at a time, did not paint a very positive picture about the outcomes of social innovations, careful reexamination of the body of literature stemming from the experimental tradition reveals the converse. That is, in the aggregate, studies show that programs have small but nontrivial positive effects on the problems they are intended to address (see Bloom, Cordray, and Light, 1988).

As with aggregated data in other scientific activities, analyses of the combined results of prior evaluations show that impact studies have contributed to our understanding of what works, for whom, and under what conditions. The problem is that this achievement requires continued support and production of high-quality, effects-oriented studies. Current trends in federal-level evaluation activities are at odds with this need, favoring instead small-scale, management-oriented studies. The types of studies conducted by OIGs contribute to this general trend.

At issue is not whether one perspective (impact versus management evaluation) is better than another, but whether the *portfolio* of evaluation activities (and, by implication, the methods) is comprehensive enough to provide competent answers to the array of oversight issues faced by managers, policymakers, the public, and other constituencies.

What Should the Evaluation Portfolio Look Like?

As a means of characterizing what the federal evaluation portfolio should look like, it is useful to think about what types of questions constituencies are likely to ask about federal expenditures on social innovations. From such a list of questions, it is a relatively simple matter to deduce evaluation criteria. So, for example, suppose the issue is whether or not continued federal action (in the form of a program) is warranted, implying that a program is already in place. The program can be evaluated on the basis of a demonstrated need for continued action, the success of its implementation, and its empirically documented impact.

Judgments on these criteria provide policymakers with a rational basis for decisions about expanding, contracting, redirecting, or eliminating a program. Obviously, if the original problem or condition that initiated a program in the first place no longer exists, there is little need to continue the program, regardless of its success with respect to impact or implementation. A program that fails to produce its intended effects, in the face of a persistent problem or condition, requires some form of alteration, revamping, or redirection.

Evaluative Criteria of the General Accounting Office (GAO)

A question-driven and action-focused perspective was behind the evaluation criteria appearing in a recent report by the GAO (U.S. General Accounting Office, 1988). Its main purpose was to provide Congress with a framework for assessing federal programs directed at children, youth, and families. Overall, its orientation is consistent with the perspectives taken by OIGs and the experimentally based, traditional program evaluation paradigm. It is far broader than either, however.

In brief, the framework encompasses a common set of program descriptors and ten evaluative subcriteria, organized under three general classes of criteria (program need, implementation, and impact). The evaluative criteria and subcategories are reproduced in Table 1. Obviously, the

**Table 1. Evaluative Criteria and
Subcriteria for Assessment of Federal Programs**

Need for the program
   Problem magnitude
   Problem seriousness
   Duplication

Implementation of the program
   Interrelationships
   Program fidelity
   Administrative efficiency

Effects of the program
   Targeting success
   Achievement of intended objectives
   Cost-effectiveness
   Other effects

Source: Adapted from U.S. General Accounting Office, 1988.

criteria imply different evaluation questions and, in turn, the need for different types of evaluation studies. For my purposes, they also provide a way of gauging the comprehensiveness of the federal-level program evaluation portfolio and, in particular, the coverage of OIG efforts. Before turning to those assessments, let me briefly define the evaluative criteria that were developed, along with a brief rationale for each.

The first group of general criteria—need for the program—is relatively straightforward. If an adverse condition exists, a corrective policy or program should be developed and installed to ameliorate the condition. Among the three evaluative subcriteria associated with program need, program magnitude concerns the importance and size of a problem, regardless of whether it exists now or can be anticipated from trends and future projections. Problems do not have to be all-encompassing in the sense that magnitude can also involve concentration of a problem by age, socioeconomic status, geographic area (urban, suburban, rural), and so on. Problem seriousness concerns the social, economic, and human consequences that might be anticipated if the problem is not addressed. And duplication focuses on whether other available resources, public or private, at the state or local levels, are sufficient to adequately address the problem. Not all problems are the same, and therefore the need for a federal program may differ within and across program areas.

The second group of general criteria examines how the program is or was carried out. As the GAO report notes, implementation includes the nature and extent of interrelationships between this program and others and what constraints or advantages are created for program operations. It also includes an assessment of program fidelity, or whether the program has been implemented as intended by Congress or the responsible federal agency, and an assessment of administrative or cost efficiency. Evidence from studies that attempt to address these issues can lead to improvements in service delivery, bolstering of the integrity of the treatment-delivery system, and corrections to the program ecology (for example, strengthening linkages among service delivery systems.).

Traditional evaluation is most commonly associated with the last set of general criteria, regarding program impact. These include whether the program has reached its intended target groups (targeting success), whether it has achieved its intended purposes, outcomes, or goals (achievement of intended objectives); how the value of these outcomes relate to the cost of producing them (cost-effectiveness), and whether the program produced effects that were unanticipated or spin-offs (either positive or negative).

This last set of criteria points out another difference between inspections and traditional program evaluations. Whereas inspections seem to focus on program operations and outcomes that can be deduced from regulations (for example, compliance reviews), criteria for success often represent the political ideologies of sponsors or critics. For example, a generic "other effect" of particular interest to the Reagan and Bush administrations concerns the extent to which programs "maintain the traditional nuclear family structure." Even though this was not an explicit, anticipated effect of many programs directed at children, youth, or families, this criterion was often raised by supporters of the Reagan administration as a benchmark for program success (and as a basis for continued support, in some instances).

These other effects are often rooted in the ideology of some constituencies and applied across programs, regardless of their original objectives. As such, evaluators must step outside the confines of formal (or, at least, written) program goals, objectives, and regulations to ascertain what other criteria are important to sectors of the policy environment.

Combining Criteria

Programs are not unidimensional. As such, evaluation criteria must be able to properly characterize the multiple attributes of social innovations. As discussed above, it is fairly obvious that by combining evidence on each of the criteria, different pictures of success emerge. Looking across the criteria, we see that impact evidence can take on a new meaning when coupled with, for example, evidence on program fidelity. Considering both of these criteria conjointly moves us away from simple descriptive claims about causality and toward explanations of how the intervention produced (or failed to produce) its intended effects. Further, careful examination of the implementation of the intervention provides valuable evidence on the micromediational mechanisms by which causes effect outcomes. That is, by devising evaluations that focus on multiple criteria, policymakers improve their ability to understand how and why programs work. Such knowledge is essential for replication and diffusion of successful programs.

Implications for the Overall Evaluation Portfolio

Obviously, comprehensive evaluation of federal programs is complex, requiring the input of diverse kinds of studies. It is unlikely that any one study, conducted by one particular group (for example, GAO or an OIG) will be able to answer all the questions implied by these criteria. Some in the evaluation and inspections professions would argue that such a "superstudy" would not be desirable on epistemological and practical (for example, political) grounds. A division of labor is needed and, indeed, is recognized by several of the authors in this volume. There is also a need for synthesis across these different types of studies. Some organizational mechanism is needed to assure that evidence is brought together in a systematic, comprehensive fashion. The details of this collaborative (or, at least, complementary) relationship among actors are not spelled out in this volume, however. Although space does not permit detailed discussion of this arena, some brief comments are warranted.

The evaluation criteria in Table 1 provide a framework for considering how a comprehensive evaluation portfolio might be established. Looking at the first set of criteria, need for the program implies the need for *ongoing* data collection. Although the United States has a rich history of monitoring economic trends (for example, housing starts, unemployment, interest rates, trade balance), it has been sporadic in its investment in monitoring important changes in the health, education, and welfare of its citizens. Reluctance to invest in data collection on the condition of education is a prime example of a reactive posture, that is, waiting until a problem is obvious (see Cordray and Datta, in press). To develop a comprehensive evaluation framework, increased attention directed at social indicators (through federal statistical units) will be needed, as opposed to only short-term, highly focused studies of the efficiency of the governmental infrastructure.

Further, judgments about the need for federal interventions also require data on the service delivery systems that are in place in local settings and on the ability of the private sector to respond to problems. The advent of block grants has, for the most part, shut off the flow of this type of community-level data. And, establishing the seriousness of a social problem will require an active, federally sponsored program of research. That is, understanding the long- and short-run consequences of adverse conditions is likely to require careful and systematic "basic" research that is not tied to a specific program evaluation study. OIG activities do not seem suited to any of these evaluative activities.

Impact studies are also not likely to be consistent with OIG structure, staffing, or expertise. Moreover, OIG emphasis on small-scale, quick turnaround, client-centered assessments can be interpreted as implying a standard that all evaluations should meet. In light of the evaluative criteria listed above, this emphasis is a mistake on several grounds. First, some of the questions, especially those devoted to assessing impact, cannot be answered in short time frames. Although this seeming lack of timeliness is often used as grounds to criticize "traditional evaluations," at issue is the precedence of accuracy over quickness in evaluating program effects.

There are often good reasons why impact assessments take longer than a couple of months or fifty staff days. Basically, many of the important problems at which federal programs are aimed involve changes in behavior that do not materialize overnight. Juvenile behavior must be examined over extended periods of time (for example, six months to one year) to ascertain whether an intervention has steered youths away from criminal activities. Evaluations of innovative cancer therapies require extended, posttherapy observation periods to assess whether survival has been lengthened, adverse side effects have been avoided, and quality of life is improved. Cross-site replications or cooperative trials designed to report aggregate data further complicate the logistics of such assessments and probably increase the amount of time needed to pull together the overall assessment. These are important evaluative questions, and a sufficient amount of time and resources should be devoted to obtaining credible answers.

Second, although evaluation specialists should be responsive to the needs of clients, responsiveness should not be measured simply as in terms of response times (for example, quick turnarounds) or answers to client-initiated questions. An important part of being responsive is educating the policymaker (or client) about the time and resource demands required to develop competent evidence on different types of questions. Until recently, we have not been particularly effective in making this point to funders and policymakers. As seen in the data of Chelimsky, Cordray, and Datta (1989) on the state of federal program evaluation in the executive branch, staff have retreated from effects-oriented studies by altering (and diluting) methods to fit time requirements and client demands. If clients do not ask the right questions, evidence bearing on many of the criteria will not be gathered, effectively closing off policy options.

Third, as evaluators and educators, we need to direct attention to the types of questions that should be addressed. To replace traditional effects-oriented evaluations with program audits or inspections because perceived time constraints permit the latter but not the former runs the risk of compressing the evaluation portfolio too narrowly. Furthermore, answering only those questions that we are asked runs the risk of answering the wrong questions. Policymakers must be educated on the types of information needed to remedy the social problem that the targeted program was intended to fix. The GAO (U.S. General Accounting Office, 1988) evaluation framework provides a useful menu from which to begin this process.

There are some natural constraints on the education process, however. Conventional wisdom suggests that evaluations should be done within time frames that are consistent with the average tenure of policymakers (short), or that they should be limited to topics that policymakers can do something about during their tenures. These constraints seem to be part of the driving force behind the inspections described in this volume and in other literature. Since impact studies and needs analyses are likely to exceed these constraints, they are seen as antithetical to the client-focused view. If this position persists, many important questions will go unanswered. Logically, a program that is well run (efficient) and exhibits limited amounts of waste, fraud, and abuse is better than one that is chaotic and wasteful. But making the next inference—that efficient and waste-free programs produce their desired effects—is just nothing more than a leap of faith. What is needed is empirical evidence, not conjecture.

The Bottom Line

OIG activities are evaluative in some ways. As such, they could be seen as complementing activities that are conducted (or should be conducted) by traditional program evaluation specialists. As far as becoming the dominant program evaluation force within the federal sector, however, they are limited in at least two ways. They focus indirectly on programs by concentrating on management issues associated with the infrastructure of the government. And, more important, OIGs cover a rather narrow set of evaluative criteria that need to be used to judge the worth of social programs.

Whereas a comprehensive set of evaluative criteria would include, at a minimum, issues of program need, implementation, and impact, inspections focus (in large measure) on administrative efficiency and a weak form of cost-effectiveness. As such, if OIGs are increasingly becoming the main players in program evaluation, a dangerous trend is developing. If that trend continues and evaluation resources (outside OIGs) continue to decline, program evaluation will be retarded rather than enhanced by the presence of OIGs. Clearly, there are issues (program need, impact, cost-effectiveness, explanation) that require far more time and technical expertise than can be accommodated by OIGs.

This work was conducted, with Stephanie Shipman, while I served as assistant director of the Program Evaluation and Methodology Division at the GAO in Washington, D.C.

References

Bloom, H. S., Cordray, D. S., and Light, R. J. (eds.). *Lessons from Selected Program and Policy Areas.* New Directions for Program Evaluation, no. 37. San Francisco: Jossey-Bass, 1988.

Chelimsky, E., Cordray, D. S., and Datta, L. G. "Federal Evaluations: The Pendulum Has Swung Too Far." *Evaluation Practice,* 1989, *10* (3), 30–36.

Cordray, D. S., and Datta, L. G. "Funding and Quality of Educational Information: Breaking the Poverty Cycle." In E. Farrar and M. Milsap (eds.), *Federal Education Policy: A Review of the 1980s.* New York: Teachers College Press, in press.

U.S. General Accounting Office. *Children's Programs: A Comparative Evaluation Framework and Five Illustrations.* Washington, D.C.: GAO/PEMD-88-28BR, 1988.

David S. Cordray is professor of public policy and psychology at Vanderbilt University, Nashville, Tennessee. He also chairs the Department of Human Resources and is a senior fellow at the Vanderbilt Institutes for Public Policy Studies.

The advent of program inspections by Offices of Inspectors General represents a departure from traditional evaluation practice. In the interest of advancing the evaluation profession, their approach deserves examination and debate by the non-OIG evaluation community.

Another View of Program Inspections by the Offices of Inspectors General

Richard C. Sonnichsen

Since the passage of the Inspector General Act in 1978, the federal evaluation landscape has been altered considerably. Not only have evaluation staffs in Health and Human Services (HHS) and the Department of Justice (DOJ) been absorbed by the Offices of Inspectors General (OIGs), but also evaluation functions in many agencies have either been discontinued or reorganized to carry out OIG audit responsibilities.

There are now OIGs in sixty-seven federal agencies, and according to Moran (this volume, p. 9), eight of these agencies have an inspections function similar to evaluation. These inspections—adaptations of audit and evaluation techniques designed to meet the needs of OIGs—are transforming the practice of evaluation in federal agencies. However, little has been published about OIG evaluation practices, even though they represent an orientation considerably different from the more traditional practice of evaluation.

Notwithstanding the dearth of information about current Inspector General (IG) evaluation methods, their methodological approaches should not be viewed negatively but instead observed objectively for potential contributions to the development of the field of evaluation.

Evaluation is a protean concept, and, like beauty, its definition and

The author thanks Gail Burton and Barbara Duffy for constructive comments on earlier drafts of this chapter. The views expressed in the chapter are the author's and do not represent the official position of the Federal Bureau of Investigation.

efficacy are in the eyes of the beholder. Its practice takes many forms, and no single definition, however broad, is likely to encompass the total range of variations. No single paradigm has been identified or agreed on by the evaluation community, nor is consensus likely in the near future. However, there are several recognized subdivisions in the evaluation landscape.

There are qualitative and quantitative evaluators, internal and external evaluators, formative and summative evaluators, and researchers and practitioners, each adapting evaluation techniques to their specific environments, educational backgrounds, training, experiences, personalities, and interests. To this diversity of practice must now be added the OIG inspections process. A recent arrival on the evaluation scene, OIG inspections are not addressed in the one hundred approaches to evaluation listed by Patton (1981).

This chapter presents one view of the OIG inspections process from an evaluation perspective, examining this emerging organizational phenomenon for its departures from traditional evaluation practice and its potential for contribution to the evaluation profession. The aim of these comments is to encourage IG evaluators to publish their experiences more widely and also to initiate a dialogue with the evaluation community in order to advance the process of evaluation.

There are considerable differences between the IG approach to evaluations and more traditional evaluation practices. In order to identify these differences, this chapter discusses the purpose, focus, and methodology of the IG evaluation process. Study of these three areas establishes that the IG inspections process is outside the mainstream procedures of the evaluation community.

Purpose of IG Evaluations

An understanding of the events leading to the establishment of OIGs is a necessary antecedent to evaluating their current performance and the dynamics that influence their behavior. The primary mission and purpose of OIGs, as set forth in the legislation and as defined by the OIGs themselves, is to prevent fraud, waste, and abuse. These terms, popularized in the 1970s and 1980s, have been used by members of Congress and by citizens to characterize accountability in governmental operations. The individuals who so eloquently drafted our Constitution failed to adequately attend to the issue of accountability and implicitly left in the hands of the executive branch of government the responsibility of accounting for federal expenditures in accordance with the law (Mosler, 1979).

The legislative history of the Inspector General Act of 1978 vividly describes the mood of Congress prior to its passage. Citing the scope of the problem and deficiencies in then-current federal efforts to combat fraud, waste, and abuse, Congress noted that "recent evidence makes it clear that fraud, waste, and abuse in the federal departments and agencies and in federally funded programs are reaching epidemic proportions" (U.S. Congress, 1978, p. 4409). Referring to organizational deficiencies, the Senate Committee on Governmental Affairs expressed the belief that "the federal government has clearly failed to make sufficient and effective efforts to prevent and detect fraud, abuse, waste, and mismanagement in federal programs and expenditures" (U.S. Congress, 1978, p. 4409).

Writing on the impact of the IG legislation, Moore and Gates (1985) cite three trends that stimulated the demand for increased government accountability: (1) a dramatic increase in the size, scope, and complexity of government operations, (2) a floundering domestic economy, and (3) a general hostility toward government.

Both Jimmy Carter and Ronald Reagan won election to the presidency on the theme that they would reduce the power and authority of the federal government and make it more manageable and accountable to the taxpayer.

The legislative history of the Inspector General Act also shows the deep concern of the members of the Senate Committee on Governmental Affairs about shocking and serious deficiencies in the auditing and investigative procedures and resources in executive branch agencies, particularly in the Department of Health, Education, and Welfare (HEW) (U.S. Congress, 1978, p. 4410). The committee found extensive fraud and abuse in HEW programs, as well as ineffective leadership and a limited number of investigators with a "ten-year backlog of un-investigated cases" (U.S. Congress, 1978, p. 4410). This concern over rampant fraud in HEW culminated in passage of the HEW Inspector General Act in 1976.

All these circumstances contributed to the passage of the 1978 Inspector General Act by a Congress frustrated with executive branch accountability. Additionally, concerned leadership in the Oval Office, coupled with a sense of growing dissatisfaction by taxpayers with the immensity of government and an apparent lack of accountability for expenditures, also served to advance the IG concept. Governmental performance would no longer be the sole purview of program managers and government executives. The statutory OIGs, empowered with extensive authority (including subpoena power) and positioned quasi-independently in the executive branch, were created to serve as governmental "watchdogs."

Clearly apparent in the events leading to the passage of the 1978 IG legislation was a palpable desire by Congress to establish rigorous accountability for appropriated funds in order to ensure that maximum value was received for all expenditures. It is significant, therefore, that the first OIG established was in HEW, the third largest budget in the world after the national government budgets of the United States and the Soviet Union.

This extreme emphasis on the funding and accountability of governmental programs has the potential to bias OIGs in both selection procedures and actual conduct of OIG evaluations. Minimally funded programs may never be subjected to oversight reviews by IG evaluators. This may be especially true if the program budgets either fall below the arbitrary funding thresholds that OIGs believe necessary to satisfy their respective congressional constituencies or are outside the scope of the internal performance goals established by OIGs to demonstrate success in identifying and preventing waste, fraud, and abuse. In this environment, formative, program-improvement evaluations may not justify diversion of resources away from more visible evaluation targets.

Focus of IG Evaluations

The bifurcated role of OIGs requires that they develop information for both the legislative and executive branches of government and for two different purposes, accountability and program improvement. This duality creates by definition an inherent conflict of interest. Which purpose has primacy? This dilemma influences evaluators throughout the evaluation process, affecting designs, data collection techniques, and reports of findings and recommendations.

Rutman (1990) argues that there are potential conflicts when program evaluation is conducted to serve both program managers' information needs and external accountability requirements. For OIGs, the information requirements of Congress vary considerably from those of executive branch program managers. The OIG program inspection approaches have their limitations and may be unable to effectively serve both masters.

Much of the time, mismanagement results from inefficiency, not from fraud or other illegalities. If specific emphasis is placed on illegal or fraudulent activities and wasteful expenditures, then the potential exists to overlook inefficient management practices. In other words, when OIGs concentrate on saving money for the taxpayer by eradicating illegal and fraudulent behavior, they may only superficially examine the management aspects of government programs. In the long run this may be more costly to the taxpayer.

Implicitly embedded in the mission of OIGs to combat waste, fraud, and abuse are two components that influence their behavior and performance: accountability and publicity. Ferreting out waste, fraud, and abuse connotes an exercise in accountability for deficiencies in program activities and service delivery. Once located, deficiencies need to be publicized to fulfill the requirement of OIGs to act as deterrents to inefficient, uneconomical, or fraudulent management practices and also to publicly demonstrate to Congress the efficacy of OIGs. This orientation may preclude assigning evaluators to low-priority programs not expected to generate congressional interest.

Enormous public programs dispensing millions of dollars to further legislative goals require not only aggressive program review activities by OIGs but also an equally aggressive publicity effort for recognition to sustain OIG activities. It is unlikely that a litany of incremental program improvements emanating from an OIG would satisfy the congressional oversight mandate in the Inspector General Act of 1978.

Illustrative of the preoccupation of OIGs with savings and recoveries are their semi-annual reports to Congress, which prominently highlight dollar savings. The OIG Office of Evaluation and Inspections at HHS claims a return on investment of two hundred dollars for every dollar expended in their budget as a result of program inspections activity. A further illustration of the importance of OIG financial savings is the emphasis, in the performance plan of the HHS deputy inspector general for evaluation and inspections, on the money his evaluations are expected to save. Explicit inclusion of a dollar-saving criterion in a plan used to judge annual performance and pay bonuses may introduce a selection bias toward big-money, high-profile targets when study requests are reviewed or OIG-initiated studies begin.

Evaluations by OIGs also exhibit a philosophical approach to program improvement different from traditional evaluations. Close observation of OIG philosophical protocol for inspections, cited by Hall and Frazier (this volume) and Moran (this volume), reveals a disquieting, militant framework that significantly departs from the more traditional, social science approach to evaluation. The IG nomenclature itself, for example, using the term "inspections" to describe what are otherwise characterized as evaluations, conveys a pugnacious nature to the entity being evaluated.

Certainly, unannounced visits by inspections teams, as described in the Department of Commerce evaluation protocol, do little to engender the cooperative spirit that evaluators attempt to develop between themselves and program managers. Depicted as a deterrent designed to increase the likelihood that Department of Commerce managers will "walk the straight and narrow," these visits tend to define the inspections process in militant terms. As reported by Moran (this volume, p. 13), the current IG for HHS views inspections as analogous to the cavalry, with inspections teams "sent out to scout the opponent's overall position in order either to engage in a limited encounter or to report back and draw up a larger battle plan." Cavalry, inspections, and unannounced visits hardly conjure up visions of evaluators and program managers cooperatively striving to understand each other's contributions to organizational effectiveness. Although a tranquil atmosphere is utopian and seldom obtained, OIG evaluation semantics, if reflective of the philosophical attitudes underlying their efforts, may do more to impede than advance the use and influence of their techniques of evaluation.

Methodological Philosophy of IG Evaluations

Evaluations conducted by OIGs are referred to as inspections and described as a variation of traditional program evaluations, designed to meet the needs of OIGs. The terms "evaluation" and "inspection" appear to be used interchangeably, but the semantic similarities of the two terms may mask deeper philosophical and theoretical differences in the nature and practices of OIG and non-OIG evaluators.

The primary tools used by OIGs to accomplish their mission are audits and investigations. The nuclei of OIG staffs, in many cases, are investigators and auditors assigned to those functions prior to the 1978 Inspector General Act. Oriented by both education and experience in accountability, these auditors and investigators have limited social science training and little disposition to view program activities from any other perspective.

Other OIG auditors and investigators have been educated and trained in the law and accounting professions and have considerable affinity for the tools of those professions to accomplish organizational goals. Davis (1990, p. 37) reports that "without doubt, the disciplinary backgrounds of program evaluation staff affect their approaches to program evaluation." He determined that auditors are more concerned with accountability than are evaluators, emphasizing management control variables, whereas program evaluators historically have concentrated on program impact measurement.

"World view" differences on how to improve the management and service delivery of government programs may impede any reconciliation between the auditor/investigator approach to program oversight and the evaluation approach of social scientists. The tools and attitudes of social scientists are developed over long periods of education, training, and experience, and they reflect a research paradigm that is not easily acquired. Changing the attitudes of persons trained in auditing procedures to a formative view of programs is an arduous task, and one that is not always satisfactorily completed.

Moreover, the necessity that OIGs remain responsive to congressional demands may impede thoughtful deliberation about evaluation design and methodological issues. Chelimsky (1990) cites the "tyranny of the legislative calendar" and the impatience of congressional policymakers as major influences on the servicing of congressional evaluation needs. Severe time pressures and an emphasis on productivity may dilute essential methodological requirements, resulting in expedient, but flawed, evaluation designs. Methodological rigor may be sacrificed for strategic political requirements to produce findings that satisfy congressional hearing deadlines.

What Can We Learn from IG Inspections?

This chapter emphasizes some of the potential pitfalls of the program inspections process. Politics, time pressures, emphasis on dollar savings, and publicity surrounding IG inspections are serious evaluation issues that have the potential to influence evaluators practicing in the OIG community. However, the existence of these conditions should not be interpreted as precluding useful, objective, defensible evaluations by OIGs. The OIG environment is simply another arena where evaluation is practiced, and we should examine the approaches and methodologies used in that arena for their benefits, deficiencies, and potential contributions to the evaluation profession.

There is little doubt that OIG evaluators enjoy a status not easily duplicated in other evaluation environments. Their statutory basis ensures independence in host organizations, and congressional interest mandates a reaction to findings and recommendations. Even without these advantages, the non-OIG evaluation community can profitably observe and learn from some of the elements of the OIG approach to evaluation practice.

There is a pragmatism in the OIG approach, a recognition that information has a utility if it is timely, relevant, and issue-oriented. With utility as a major criterion for judging the performance of OIG program inspections, we must place them in the category of evaluations that are actually used by the intended clients (Patton, 1986). So while this chapter has concentrated on purpose, focus, and methodology as three areas of departure from the traditional practice of evaluation, these adaptations paradoxically also represent some of the reasons that OIG evaluations are publicized and utilized. The challenge for the OIG and non-OIG evaluation communities is thus to (1) acknowledge each other's presence, (2) recognize that there is more than one approach to evaluation, and (3) initiate a dialogue that will open and sustain communication and sharing between the two groups to the benefit of all evaluators.

The OIGs seem to be interested in developing a relationship with the evaluation community and in receiving recognition for their evaluation work. This volume is one example of that interest. Another example is the letter to American Evaluation Association (AEA) members from HHS Inspector General Richard Kusserow, conveying his disappointment at not being able to address the 1989 AEA convention because of the San Francisco earthquake. In his letter he announced that his Office of Analysis and Inspections would henceforth be known as the Office of Evaluation and Inspections. Kusserow stated that inclusion of the term "evaluation" in this office's title was designed to "more correctly describe our activity and, quite frankly, to move ourselves closer to the evaluation community in general" (Kusserow, personal letter to American Evaluation Association conferees, Dec. 27, 1989).

Auditing, evaluation, and inspections are not mutually exclusive endeavors but rather variations of organizational review functions. By bridging the differences among the three activities and adopting the efficacious components of each, an improved evaluation product may emerge. Chelimsky (1990) observes that once we understand the different perspectives and approaches between auditors and evaluators, opportunities appear for valuable interchange.

Inasmuch as OIGs are carving a niche in the field of evaluation that is result-oriented and effective, their inspections reports inform the public debate by being relevant, credible, understandable, and timely. OIGs have recognized that timeliness is a touchstone for evaluators wishing to contribute to the decision-making process within an organization.

Operating under the assumption that public administrators will make decisions, with or without empirical data, OIG inspections programs strive to publish their inspections reports in advance of policy debate deadlines, thus maximizing the potential for utilization. This advocacy approach to ensuring that inspections findings are included in public debates is a departure from the traditional, academic, neutral evaluation approach. But it is an effective counterweight to the ubiquitous lament in the evaluation literature that evaluation reports are rarely used (Sonnichsen, 1988).

Weaknesses exist in any approach to evaluation, and successful evaluators must maintain their personal and professional standards while adapting to the requirements of diverse situations. The program inspections approach to evaluations has balanced epistemological considerations with the pragmatism of public policy development. There may not always be sufficient time to assure methodological elegance, but delays in meeting evaluation deadlines may impede timely information flow from evaluators to decision makers, rendering a disservice to both parties. The program inspections approach to evaluation practice recognizes information as a commodity with a limited shelf life. Failure to respond to organizational deadlines for decision making diminishes the utility of evaluations.

Clearly, OIGs have an advantage by combining organizational independence with organizational knowledge. Independence is always an issue for internal evaluation offices (House, 1986, 1988, 1989; Sonnichsen, 1987, 1989). However, the unique status of OIGs, with their independence legislatively guaranteed, allows them to concentrate on other evaluation issues confronting internal evaluation offices, without devoting any energy to defending their independence.

Acquiring knowledge about the OIGs' methodological and philosophical approaches to evaluation is a beneficial endeavor and should be pursued by non-OIG evaluators. It would be a disservice to the development and refinement of the evaluation profession to isolate the OIG community from the traditional evaluation arena due to a parochial perspective by "mainstream" evaluators that OIGs practice a "different" type of evaluation. This posture contributes nothing to the dialogue and, in fact, impedes the development of the evaluation profession.

Summary

The OIG evaluation community should neither be chastised for their inspections process nor ignored by mainstream evaluators. Instead, they should be viewed as another approach among the many options now employed to review organizational activities. No claim of superiority for one version of evaluation over another is sustainable, and all such claims are clearly inappropriate. Creating a dialogue with OIG evaluators can contribute to a better understanding of their environment and to further development of the field of evaluation. The idiosyncratic nature of organizations and programs calls for a diversity of approaches to evaluation and a pluralistic philosophical orientation to the evaluation of government programs. Inviting and encouraging participation by OIG evaluators in AEA activities and local evaluation organizations can promote an exchange of ideas and a sharing of experiences, fostering beneficial outcomes for both groups while strengthening the evaluation profession.

Evaluation, stripped of its jargon and fixation on methodological subtleties, essentially aims to produce information about how programs work and their effectiveness in alleviating the problems they are designed to cure (Sonnichsen, 1990). With this premise in mind, the evaluation profession ought to encourage any systematic review of programs that use evaluation to improve government services. No single evaluation approach can accomplish this goal, and all opportunities for professional development need to be examined for their potential contribution to this goal. Evaluation, as practiced by OIGs, deserves this attention.

References

Chelimsky, E. "Expanding GAO's Capabilities in Program Evaluation." *GAO Journal,* 1990, *8,* 43-52.

Davis, D. F. "Do You Want a Performance Audit or a Program Evaluation?" *Public Administration Review,* 1990, *50* (1), 35-41.

House, E. R. "Internal Evaluation." *Evaluation Practice,* 1986, *7* (1), 63-64.

House, E. R. "Evaluating the FBI: A Response to Sonnichsen." *Evaluation Practice,* 1988, *9* (3), 43-46.

House, E. R. "Response to Richard Sonnichsen." *Evaluation Practice,* 1989, *10* (3), 64-65.

Moore, M. H., and Gates, M. J. "Junkyard Dogs and Wise-Old Dogs: A Preliminary Investigation of Inspectors-General in the Federal Government." Unpublished manuscript, Harvard University, John F. Kennedy School of Government, 1985.

Mosler, F. C. *The GAO: The Quest for Accountability in American Government.* Boulder, Colo.: Westview Press, 1979.

Patton, M. Q. *Creative Evaluation.* Newbury Park, Calif.: Sage, 1981.

Patton, M. Q. *Utilization-Focused Evaluation.* Newbury Park, Calif.: Sage, 1986.

Rutman, L. "Serving Management and Accountability: A Conflict for Program Evaluation?" *Evaluation Practice,* 1990, *11* (1), 39-43.

Sonnichsen, R. C. "An Internal Evaluator Responds to Ernest House's Views on Internal Evaluation." *Evaluation Practice,* 1987, *8* (4), 34-36.

Sonnichsen, R. C. "Advocacy Evaluation: A Model for Internal Evaluation Offices." *Evaluation and Program Planning,* 1988, *11,* 141-148.

Sonnichsen, R. C. "An Open Letter to Ernest House." *Evaluation Practice,* 1989, *10* (3), 59-63.

Sonnichsen, R. C. "Evaluation as Organizational Learning." In C. Bellavita (ed.), *How Public Organizations Work: Lessons from Experience.* New York: Praeger, 1990.

U.S. Congress. Senate. *Congressional Record.* 95th Cong. 2d sess., 1978. Vol. 124, p. 4406-4410.

Richard C. Sonnichsen is the deputy assistant director of the Federal Bureau of Investigation, in charge of the Office of Planning, Evaluation, and Audits. He is a doctoral candidate in public administration at the University of Southern California, Los Angeles.

INDEX

Adoptions, evaluation of, 28
Advocacy evaluation, by OIGs, 2, 84
Agency for International Development, OIG in, 12
Aid to Families with Dependent Children (AFDC), evaluation of, 33, 34
American Behavioral Scientist, 33
American Evaluation Association (AEA), 83, 85; standards of, 18, 32
American Journal of Epidemiology, 33
American Society for Public Administration, Elmer B. Staats Award for Program Evaluation of, 25
Armed Forces Institute of Pathology, inspection of, 52, 59-60
Armed Forces Medical Museum, inspection of, 52
Audits, 1, 2, 11, 28, 50; definition of, 13; by OIGs, 12, 17, 82. *See also* General Accounting Office

Block grants, 10, 73
Bloom, H. S., 69, 75
Briefings, conduct of, 32, 44, 48
Budget: federal, 10; HHS, 27, 79
Bureau of the Census, inspection of, 42
The Bureaucrat, 33
Bush administration, 15, 72

Califano, J. A., Jr., 26-27
Cancer therapies, evaluation of, 73-74
Carter, J., 26, 79
Casey, J. H., 54, 61
Center for Advanced Education, inspection of, 52
Central Intelligence Agency, OIG in, 1
Champion, H., 26-27
Chelimsky, E., 2, 4, 68, 74, 82, 83, 85
Cheney, D., 53, 61
Child support, evaluation of, 34
Colson, C., 49, 61
Community Services Administration, OIG in, 12
Compliance reviews, 13, 56
Computer technology, and evaluations, 28-30, 34, 42, 56

Computer-assisted telephone interviewing, 30
Concept plan, 54-56, 58
Congressional set-asides, 68-69
Contractors, outside, 10, 15
Cordray, D. S., 4, 68, 69, 73, 74, 75
Cost-benefit analyses, 56
Cost-savings, by OIGs, 15-16, 33-34, 45, 67, 81
Criminal investigations, by OIGs, 1, 39

Data collection and analysis, 29, 31, 44, 73
Datta, L. G., 68, 73, 74, 75
Davis, D. F., 82, 85
Defense Communications Agency, inspection of, 55
Defense Fiscal Year 1990 Authorization Act, 53
Defense Intelligence Agency, inspection of, 51, 53
Defense Investigative Service, inspection of, 60
Defense Logistics Agency, 50-51
Defense Mapping Agency, inspection of, 50, 53, 60
Defense Personnel Support Center, inspection of, 55
Deputy secretary of Defense, 57

Environmental Protection Agency, OIG in, 12
Essential Elements of Information (EEI), 54
Evaluation, comprehensive, 69, 75
Evaluation, traditional, 10-11; versus inspections, 15-16, 65-75, 81-82

Federal agencies, with OIGs, 13-14
Federal Bureau of Investigation (FBI), OIG in, 2
Federal Emergency Management Agency, OIG in, 12
Focus groups, as evaluation technique, 30
Fraud, waste, and abuse, inspections for, 10, 40, 43, 46, 50, 66, 78, 80-81. *See also* Inspector General Act of 1978
Frazier, J., 3, 37-48, 81

ORDERING INFORMATION

NEW DIRECTIONS FOR PROGRAM EVALUATION is a series of paperback books that presents the latest techniques and procedures for conducting useful evaluation studies of all types of programs. Books in the series are published quarterly in Fall, Winter, Spring, and Summer and are available for purchase by subscription as well as by single copy.

SUBSCRIPTIONS for 1990 cost $48.00 for individuals (a savings of 20 percent over single-copy prices) and $70.00 for institutions, agencies, and libraries. Please do not send institutional checks for personal subscriptions. Standing orders are accepted.

SINGLE COPIES cost $15.95 when payment accompanies order. (California, New Jersey, New York, and Washington, D.C., residents please include appropriate sales tax.) Billed orders will be charged postage and handling.

DISCOUNTS FOR QUANTITY ORDERS are available. Please write to the address below for information.

ALL ORDERS must include either the name of an individual or an official purchase order number. Please submit your order as follows:
Subscriptions: specify series and year subscription is to begin
Single copies: include individual title code (such as PE1)

MAIL ALL ORDERS TO:
Jossey-Bass Inc., Publishers
350 Sansome Street
San Francisco, California 94104

FOR SALES OUTSIDE OF THE UNITED STATES CONTACT:
Maxwell Macmillan International Publishing Group
866 Third Avenue
New York, New York 10022

OTHER TITLES AVAILABLE IN THE
NEW DIRECTIONS FOR PROGRAM EVALUATION SERIES
Nick L. Smith, *Editor-in-Chief*